LITERACY IN A PLC AT WORK®

Guiding Teams to Get Going and Get Better in Grades K–6 Reading

PAULA MAEKER AND JACQUELINE HELLER

Solution Tree | Press

a division of
Solution Tree

555 North Morton Street
Bloomington, IN 47404
800.733.6786 (toll free) / 812.336.7700
FAX: 812.336.7790

email: info@SolutionTree.com
SolutionTree.com

Visit **go.SolutionTree.com/literacy** to download the free reproducibles in this book.

Printed in the United States of America

Library of Congress Cataloging-in-Publication Data

Names: Maeker, Paula, author. | Heller, Jacqueline, author.
Title: Literacy in a PLC at work : guiding teams to get going and get
    better in grades K-6 reading / Paula Maeker, Jacqueline Heller.
Other titles: Literacy in a professional learning communities at work
Description: Bloomington, IN : Solution Tree Press, [2023] | Includes
    bibliographical references and index.
Identifiers: LCCN 2023007924 (print) | LCCN 2023007925 (ebook) | ISBN
    9781949539585 (paperback) | ISBN 9781951075538 (ebook)
Subjects: LCSH: Literacy--Study and teaching (Elementary)--United States. |
    Professional learning communities--United States. | Elementary school
    teachers--In-service training--United States. | School improvement
    programs--United States. | Group work in education--United States. |
    Team learning approach in education--United States. | Educational
    change--United States. | Educational leadership--United States.
Classification: LCC LC151 .M24 2023 (print) | LCC LC151 (ebook) | DDC
    372.6--dc23/eng/20230313
LC record available at https://lccn.loc.gov/2023007924
LC ebook record available at https://lccn.loc.gov/2023007925

Solution Tree
Jeffrey C. Jones, CEO
Edmund M. Ackerman, President

Solution Tree Press
President and Publisher: Douglas M. Rife
Associate Publishers: Todd Brakke and Kendra Slayton
Editorial Director: Laurel Hecker
Art Director: Rian Anderson
Copy Chief: Jessi Finn
Senior Production Editor: Tonya Maddox Cupp
Copy Editor: Jessi Finn
Proofreader: Evie Madsen
Text and Cover Designer: Fabiana Cochran
Acquisitions Editor: Hilary Goff
Assistant Acquisitions Editor: Elijah Oates
Content Development Specialist: Amy Rubenstein
Associate Editor: Sarah Ludwig
Editorial Assistant: Anne Marie Watkins

Acknowledgments

This book is for the women in my life who have taught me to be brave. My list begins with my two favorite women, Elizabeth Schultz, a World War II veteran, and the most amazing model of unconditional love I've known, and Allison Maeker, whose authenticity, creativity, and kindness are marvels. The list of courageous women continues with my sister, my friends, my colleagues and mentors, my students, and especially my coauthor (who also ranks high in the friend category). Thank you, Jacquie, for inviting me on this journey. This is also for Mark and Jake, the two men in my life who have never failed to honor women's voices and have endlessly encouraged me to raise mine. You are all deeply part of who I am. Your hearts and minds have shaped me, challenged me, and lifted me up. I could not be more grateful. —Paula

To my husband, Tommy, who was reading to our twin babies in the NICU all those years ago: your ceaseless support has challenged me to thrive and grow every day since then. To Griffith and Tessa, those preemie babies who grew beyond my wildest expectations into phenomenal humans: your impact on this world inspires me to keep writing in order to increase my own impact. To the unparalleled staff at Mason Crest Elementary School and the literacy leaders in Fairfax County Public Schools who had the most profound impact on my own professional development: I hope you are proud to see the ripples of our collective experiences in these pages. To the teams of teachers everywhere, but especially across Arkansas, who are willing to roll up their sleeves and constantly refine their literacy practices because they are so invested in the success of their students: you are my heroes. To all those behind the scenes at Solution Tree who enable that work to happen in schools and have shaped how Paula and I capture that work in this text: thank you for your vision. To my coauthor partner, Paula: your passion has transformed this journey and this educator in the best of ways. To Rick and Becky: we are so honored to be your legacy. —Jacquie

We, Jacquie and Paula, would like to thank our colleagues who are passionate literacy practitioners and educational leaders and who took time to offer their insights and support as peer reviewers: Casey Ahner, Katie Atkins, Anisa Baker-Busby, Brian Butler, Martha Curiel, Kelli Fuller, Amy Henchey, Chris Jakicic, Cheryl Kelley, Lyndsay Rogers, and Matthew Treadway. We are so grateful to learn from and with all of you.

Solution Tree Press would like to thank the following reviewers:

Connie Debes
    Kindergarten Teacher
    Lincoln Consolidated Schools
    Lincoln, Arkansas

Justin Green
    Third-Grade Teacher; President Elect—
    Canadian Assessment for Learning
        Network
    Nanaimo Ladysmith Public Schools
    Nanaimo, British Columbia, Canada

Erin Kruckenberg
    Fifth-Grade Teacher
    Harvard Community Unit School
        District 50
    Harvard, Illinois

Jane Losinger
    District Supervisor of Language Arts
        Literacy
    Howell Township Public Schools
    Howell, New Jersey

Sarah Svendsen
    Instructional Coach, Kindergarten
        Teacher
    Pine Crest School
    Boca Raton, Florida

Rachel Swearengin
    Fifth-Grade Teacher
    Manchester Park Elementary School
    Olathe, Kansas

Visit **go.SolutionTree.com/literacy** to download the free reproducibles in this book.

Table of Contents

Reproducibles are in italics.

About the Authors

 **P**aula Maeker is an educator, consultant, and advocate for learner-centered education. She has more than twenty-three years' experience as an elementary teacher, literacy specialist, instructional coach, Title I program coordinator, campus administrator, director of elementary literacy, and director of instructional design. Paula most recently served as director of instructional design for Tomball Independent School District in northwest Houston, Texas.

Much of Paula's career has been spent serving high-needs campuses as a literacy teacher and instructional coach. She specializes in multitiered systems of support, acceleration models, building collaborative teams, coaching leadership through the professional-learning-for-all culture, using assessment to inform teaching practices, and creating effective instructional frameworks to guarantee high levels of learning for every student.

Paula has been named Teacher of the Year and Professional of the Year and received many other local honors and awards, including an H-E-B Texas Excellence in Education Award nomination. She also served at three highly collaborative schools that each earned a national Model Professional Learning Community (PLC) School designation and has proudly supported many more schools in earning that recognition.

She completed her undergraduate studies at the University of Alabama at Birmingham and received her master of education in school administration from Lamar University in Beaumont, Texas. She holds Texas principal, master reading teacher preK–12, generalist EC–4, and English as a second language K–12 teaching certifications.

Jacqueline Heller focuses on building capacity and collective efficacy with teachers to ensure all students learn at high levels. Jacquie has extensive experience leading teams to collaborate around data-driven instruction, spending most of her twenty-five-year career working with Title 1 schools and learning from diverse language learners and students living in poverty.

As a reading recovery teacher, Title I teacher, and reading resource teacher, she partnered with the teachers of hundreds of students who had experienced initial reading challenges and helped them develop the skills students needed to see themselves as fluent readers. As a literacy teacher and instructional coach, she helped Mason Crest Elementary School in Annandale, Virginia, become the first national Model PLC to receive the DuFour Award, which recognizes the highest-performing PLC from around the globe.

Jacquie coauthored the book *What About Us? The PLC at Work® Process for Grades PreK–2 Teams* and has been published in the *Journal of Literacy Research*. She has presented at the state, national, and international levels. After being part of the leadership teams that transformed two elementary schools in Fairfax County, Virginia, into national Model PLCs, she began consulting with schools across the United States, and has coached many more schools in doing the work to improve student learning and receive Model PLC designations.

She received a bachelor of science degree from the University of Virginia and a master of education degree from George Mason University, where she went on to do further graduate work in literacy and change management.

To book Paula Maeker or Jacqueline Heller for professional development, contact pd@SolutionTree.com.

Introduction

If you don't see the book
you want on the shelves, write it.

—Beverly Cleary

Literacy is the core of elementary education. We (Jacquie and Paula) often hear elementary teachers say of all the content they teach, they are least comfortable with or confident in their literacy instruction because there is so much they *could* do and so many directions they *could* take in reading instruction, but they are not sure where to start. We recognize how difficult that can be.

That is one reason we wrote this book. There are other reasons, but at the heart of it is the fact that we are practitioners with a shared mission, which is, *We believe all students can be literate at high levels, and it is our work that ensures equitable outcomes for all.* This call to action drives us to provide equitable literacy outcomes for every student we serve and now drives the purpose, focus, and passion behind the tools, resources, and learning shared in this book.

While the following chapters hopefully propel elementary teams to reflect on their current practices in reading, we contend that learning about reading through the lens of the Professional Learning Community (PLC) at Work® process will also help you think through other topics in education that you or your school may be grappling with as problems of practice in 21st century literacy. If you've been engaged in discussions about topics such as culturally relevant instruction, social-emotional learning, effective grading practices, and equity in education, know that the work we propose is not a competing agenda, but instead a framework for how teams can better sustain change and improve their practices as literacy educators. As teams engage in the process outlined in each chapter, they will find opportunities to integrate these considerations. For example, when choosing resources to support essential learning, teams may intentionally select culturally relevant texts to support an inclusive understanding of others. This also allows students to see themselves represented in empowering and inspiring ways. As teams utilize the protocols, there is space for thoughtful discussions about how to highlight social-emotional learning by designing opportunities for students to engage in text-to-self connections, which build understanding of relationships and emotions. This framework also guides teams in providing effective feedback and grading practices designed to build students' confidence, efficacy, and motivation. If teams embrace the mission to ensure equitable outcomes for every literacy learner, then equity is the beneficiary of the process.

Before we dive into the framework, we will give some background on how we have engaged in this work and how you may benefit from engaging in this work with us.

Finding Joy in the Journey

We, both Jacquie and Paula, spent a couple of decades as elementary classroom teachers and then literacy specialists in high-needs schools where we were driven to change the trajectory of students' lives by cracking the code of what each individual student needed to become literate. Before we met, at one point in each of our careers, we also worked in and led schools and districts that realized even the greatest of teachers cannot change the trajectory of so many students' lives on their own. That can only happen for all students when teacher teams take collective responsibility for learning, specifically target what students need to learn, and use data to analyze results, inform instruction, and improve teacher practices. In other words, we had the great fortune to build schools that embraced the PLC at Work process. That is when we started to believe we could bring our mission to life. Through dedication, hard work, and strong systems and structures, our schools became nationally recognized Model PLCs (by demonstrating commitment to culture and structures of the PLC at Work process as well as providing evidence of significant student achievement for at least three years). Educators from around the world visited to understand how to replicate the process to positively impact student achievement.

Having stepped away from our districts (Paula in Texas and Jacquie in Virginia), we both work with teams across the United States to bring them the understandings and tools they need to get better reading outcomes for young scholars. It is our grandest desire to ensure every student can live a life of limitless possibilities, so our work is to help every teacher team bring high levels of literacy to all students. Every single one. That journey starts with reading instruction in the early years of school, so that is where this book begins.

This topic happens to be the ultimate intersection of our two professional passions, PLCs and literacy, so you will hear our voice coming through with a sense of urgency. We truly believe our students do not have any time for us to waste. We know this is hard, messy work, and while there will be moments when teams will face and embrace struggle, they will also find humor and celebrations along the way. We've lived it and assure you there is joy in the journey.

Joining the Journey

This book will help grades K–6 literacy teachers, interventionists, and instructional coaches understand how collaborative teams prioritize the most essential learning in order to develop capable readers. It will also help teams understand how to best make those decisions by working in the context of a PLC at Work.

Some readers may already have a deep understanding of aspects of literacy but be new practitioners of the PLC concept, while others may know the work of the PLC process well and be seeking new tools to strengthen their collaborative literacy practices. Read on—we've got you both! This practical guide will help you replicate the work we do with teams when we are on site transforming schools into high-functioning collaborative teams working the PLC process with greatly improved literacy practices and the student reading achievement results to prove it.

Defining Literacy

What exactly do we mean by *literacy*? A comprehensive literacy instructional block includes reading, writing, word study, listening, and speaking. In this book, we focus only on the reading instruction—but that does not simplify it much, because the National Reading Panel (2000) identifies the following critical components that reading itself must address.

- **Phonemic awareness:** The ability to manipulate individual sounds in spoken words (*phonemes*) and recognize, identify, categorize, blend, segment, and omit phonemes orally (Reading Rockets, n.d.b)

- **Phonics:** Learning how to apply knowledge of letter-sound correspondences and spelling patterns to decode written words (Hasbrouck, n.d.)

- **Fluency:** The ability to read text accurately, at a proper rate, with appropriate expression (Reading Rockets, n.d.b)

- **Vocabulary:** Knowledge of words and their meanings (Butler et al., 2010)

- **Comprehension:** A reader's constructed meaning through interactions with text (Paris & Hamilton, 2014)

Consider your current practices, curriculum, and focus of instruction. Does your reading curriculum address each of the needs of your learners as defined here? Does your team prioritize the time in your literacy instructional block to develop the concepts most important for higher reading proficiency?

The first two concepts, phonemic awareness and phonics, are often emphasized more in the kindergarten and early elementary years, with the emphasis shifting to the last two concepts, vocabulary and comprehension, after students become fluent readers. But K–6 teachers have students reading above and, often, far below grade level, so they must all have a depth of knowledge about each of the five components.

Making Peace With the Reading Wars

We are extremely lucky to serve and support literacy teams all over, so we have seen many iterations of successful instruction. While we may find differing ideas and practices around the *balanced literacy* or *science of reading* approach in different schools and districts, at the end of the day teachers can all agree that the craft of teaching reading is difficult and complex work. Given the recurring debates that continue to pop up in social media, the news, blogs, and legislation, we believe it is important to address some of the thinking around these debates.

The simplified version of the reading wars is that there are differing views on how best to engage students in literacy instruction, and historically, these deeply held beliefs have developed as camps with little room for compromise in adopting the ideas and practices of the others. The whole language approach is a view that hearkens back as far as 150 years ago (Kim, 2008). *Whole language* followers think that the best method in teaching reading is to instruct students to recognize words as whole pieces of meaning, believing that "language should not be broken down into letters and combinations of letters and 'decoded'" (Reading Horizons, n.d.). They believe that "language is a complete system of making meaning, with words functioning in relation to each other in context" (Reading Horizons, n.d.). This whole language approach emphasizes experiences within texts rather than breaking reading into specific skills such as phonics to be taught in isolation.

In opposition to the whole language approach, *phonics-based reading* instruction gained popularity in the late 1950s after research was introduced to question the effectiveness of the whole language approach (Kim, 2008). Phonics instruction includes teaching young students to read and spell words by applying the letter-sound combinations to "decode words based on their spellings. Phonics attempts to break written language down into small and simple components" (Reading Horizons, n.d.).

By the 1990s, the debate became so heated that the U.S. federal government stepped in and created a National Reading Panel to conduct research and report its findings to end the reading wars. Enter the *balanced literacy* approach (National Reading Panel, 2000), which was intended to be the perfect marriage of phonics-based instruction and whole language experiences by teaching phonics and other skills students need to read in a meaning-making context with real texts (Bingham & Hall-Kenyon, 2013). Balanced literacy practitioners are supposed to strike a balance of phonemic awareness, phonics, fluency, vocabulary, and comprehension, and they use a wide variety of strategies and instructional methods to achieve reading goals (Reading Horizons, n.d.).

You would think that the bridge created with the actual word *balance* in the description would have brought peace and harmony in the land of literacy, but no. As with many things in life, striking the right balance was very difficult, so practitioners questioned how to prioritize and teach each component, which brought even more confusion, debate, and partisanship. The national dialogue around reading shifted again as research in neuroscience backed those in the phonics camp (Shanahan, 2020). That research armed them to deepen the cracks in the balanced literacy framework and sway many practitioners and teacher preparation programs to reconsider their approach and embrace more systematic, explicit skill-based reading instruction with a strong foundation in phonemic awareness and phonics. Those who just want to know how to help more students read better have been caught in the fray and left frustrated, overwhelmed, and questioning what to believe.

Here's what we consider to be an absolute truth: teaching reading *effectively* is downright complicated. We also know that teachers are some of the most passionate, dedicated professionals on the planet. As practitioners, we are still students of literacy, as well. We're smart enough to know that we don't know everything about teaching and learning reading. It's better to resolve to be in perpetual professional learning mode and apply the best of what we have with everything we've got. This book is designed to support teams in that process.

We want to stop here and eliminate the question of whether the PLC at Work process will fit within the framework of any chosen side of the reading wars. The short answer is it absolutely will. Undeniably. The long answer is outlined in the chapters ahead as practically and as simply as possible.

We find that the reading wars waged among the competing philosophies or approaches have become a distraction to the work of literacy teams. How do team members find common ground? The following data should rally team members to come together with unparalleled urgency for the shared goal of improving student achievement in reading.

- Only 35 percent of U.S. fourth graders are proficient in reading (National Center for Education Statistics [NCES], 2022).

- Only 21 percent of low-income students in the United States are proficient in reading (NCES, 2022).

- Thirty-seven percent of high school seniors in the United States are proficient in reading (NCES, 2022).

- Fifty-four percent of U.S. adults sixteen to seventy-four years old cannot read proficiently (Nietzel, 2020).

- Twenty percent of U.S. adults are not able to read proficiently enough to earn a living wage (Orton Gillingham Online Academy, 2017).

- In Australia, almost 44 percent of adults read at or below a secondary proficiency level (Australian Bureau of Statistics, 2013).

- In Canada, about half of adults could not pass a high school–level reading assessment (Statistics Canada, 2015).

Whether looking at reading instruction through the lens of whole to part or part to whole, collectively team members have to find a way to guide students to and through high levels of literacy. The PLC at Work process has a preponderance of evidence to back up its claim of improving student learning (DuFour, DuFour, Eaker, Many, & Mattos, 2016). So instead of focusing on a particular instructional methodology, this book centers on utilizing the PLC at Work process to address reading standards as outlined in local, state, provincial, or federal guidelines. We want to address how teams collaboratively engage in ensuring all students learn at high levels of literacy, not impose instructional pedagogy. Throughout this book, we honor the thinking, practices, and pedagogy of research-based reading philosophies and programs because at the end of the day, our work is to guarantee that all students receive tools, strategies, skills, and mindsets based on their individual needs. When teams engage in the collaborative process, capable readers emerge. Here's the thing—we believe that the only reading war we should be fighting is the war against illiteracy.

Among our beliefs is that no one can transform literacy achievement in more powerful and impactful ways than teacher teams. It's our moral imperative, call to arms, and sleeves-rolled-up, ready-to-work motivator. Imagine if educators rallied to eradicate inequities that occur because of an education system that wasn't designed to meet the needs of all learners. Just think about if all elementary teachers of literacy worked in a collaborative framework and structure that guarantees every single student they serve will read at or above proficiency expectations. Educators must respond as if students' lives depend on it, because now more than ever, in more ways than you may know, they do.

> Here's the thing—we believe that the only reading war we should be fighting is the war against illiteracy.

Understanding the Professional Learning Community at Work Process

Let's begin by ensuring a common understanding about the characteristics of a true team of collaborators who do the work within the PLC process. PLC is defined as "an ongoing process in which educators work collaboratively in recurring cycles of collective inquiry and action research to achieve better results for the students they serve" (DuFour et al., 2016, p. 10).

Let's dig a little deeper and seek clarity on some of this definition's key ideas.

> "... an **ongoing** process ..." *We commit to continuously improving.*

This isn't a quick fix or boxed program wrapped in cellophane that promises results if used with fidelity. This is a doable process that drives reading outcomes forward. We educators do the hard work of determining where we are, set goals for where we want to be, and make an actionable plan to get there. Then we set off on the journey and keep making stops along the way for directions.

"... educators work **collaboratively** ..." *We commit to taking a team approach and to holding each other mutually accountable for reaching our collective goals.*

If our mission is to ensure every student learns at high levels in literacy, then it stands to reason that it is not humanly possible for a single teacher working in isolation to be able to make that happen. There are hundreds of proverbs spanning centuries, cultures, and continents that have taught us about the power of collaboration. These include, for example, "Many hands make light work," "It takes a village to raise a child," and "Are you crazy? There is no way I can get twenty-six first graders to on-grade-level mastery in reading all by myself!"

"... cycles of **collective inquiry** ..." *We commit to being learners.*

Seeking information means you are learning. And the true power of this process is that the professionals work together to get better at the craft of teaching reading. They work together to analyze systems, structures, practices, pedagogy, thinking, and data to determine what works and what doesn't. This study of teaching and learning anchors our collaboration in a common language, understanding, and purpose. We may never have all the right answers as literacy educators, but in the PLC at Work process, teams refuse to stop asking the right questions.

"... **action research** ..." *We commit to putting our work into practice.*

Research is studying something in detail in order to reach a new understanding (Research, n.d.), but action research links understanding with practice, application, and reflection. The words *by doing* are crucial to our work—not just thinking about it, talking about it, or sitting in a literacy workshop, but learning about it. We actually put our learning into action. Others will see us *behaving* it. We also monitor the effectiveness of our policies, procedures, and practices and are focused on results, not assumptions or intentions.

"... **better results** for the students ..." *We commit to ensuring all students learn at high levels.*

Isn't this why we exist? In fact, the first big idea of the PLC at Work process (see later text in this section for clarification on the three big ideas) is that we embrace learning as our fundamental purpose (DuFour et al., 2016). We don't dedicate our hearts and souls to the very difficult work of teaching and learning in literacy for some of our students to do OK in reading some of the time. When we implement the PLC process, we relentlessly commit to make high levels of literacy learning happen for every student.

> "... they **serve**." *We commit to aligning our beliefs and behaviors in service of our purpose.*

Serve is perhaps our favorite word in the definition. Our late colleague and mentor, Rebecca DuFour, often shared a poem by Marge Piercy (1982) to remind us of our mission, purpose, and promise of this work. That poem is simply titled "To Be of Use." Why serve? To be of use. We're going to leave that right there.

But consider the three, four, and five.

- The **three big ideas** of a PLC at Work
- The **four pillars** of a PLC at Work
- The **five tight elements** of a PLC at Work

To function with fidelity as collaborative teams according to the definition of the PLC process requires a mindset shift in how educators think about literacy instruction and cultural shifts in how they work as a team. They move from engaging in *teaching* reading as individual educators to collectively ensuring their students are *learning* to read. When educators embrace literacy teaching and learning through the lens of the PLC at Work process, they commit fully to the following three big ideas of a PLC (DuFour et al., 2016). Consider the application of these three big ideas to literacy in figure I.1.

Big Idea One: A Focus on Learning
We work collaboratively to ensure all students reach high levels of proficiency in reading.
We ensure all educators are building shared knowledge of effective literacy instructional practices through job-embedded learning.
Big Idea Two: A Culture of Collaboration and Collective Responsibility
We build a collaborative system and process that requires us to work interdependently to build shared knowledge and achieve our shared literacy goals.
We take collective responsibility and hold each other mutually accountable for our shared goals in literacy.
Big Idea Three: A Results Orientation
We are reflective practitioners constantly seeking evidence of effectiveness in literacy practices and achievement.
We analyze everything we do based on the impact on students' literacy learning.

Source: Adapted from DuFour et al., 2016.

FIGURE I.1: Application of the three big ideas of a PLC at Work to literacy.

Teams need a structure to align their work with these three big ideas. *Learning by Doing: A Handbook for Professional Learning Communities at Work* (DuFour et al., 2016) shares four critical questions of learning that drive the work of ensuring all students learn at high levels (we love the double meaning of the term *critical* because the questions are imperative and require complex thinking). We've included the anchor terms *know, show, grow,* and *glow* as a cue to help teams understand the purpose and intention of each of the four critical questions in figure I.2.

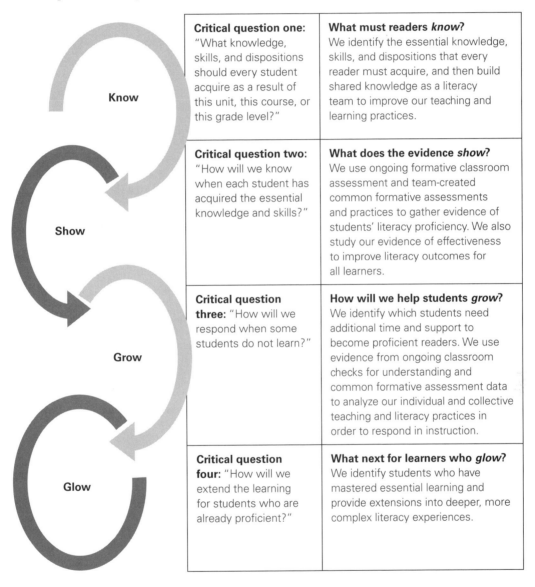

Know	**Critical question one:** "What knowledge, skills, and dispositions should every student acquire as a result of this unit, this course, or this grade level?"	**What must readers *know*?** We identify the essential knowledge, skills, and dispositions that every reader must acquire, and then build shared knowledge as a literacy team to improve our teaching and learning practices.
Show	**Critical question two:** "How will we know when each student has acquired the essential knowledge and skills?"	**What does the evidence *show*?** We use ongoing formative classroom assessment and team-created common formative assessments and practices to gather evidence of students' literacy proficiency. We also study our evidence of effectiveness to improve literacy outcomes for all learners.
Grow	**Critical question three:** "How will we respond when some students do not learn?"	**How will we help students *grow*?** We identify which students need additional time and support to become proficient readers. We use evidence from ongoing classroom checks for understanding and common formative assessment data to analyze our individual and collective teaching and literacy practices in order to respond in instruction.
Glow	**Critical question four:** "How will we extend the learning for students who are already proficient?"	**What next for learners who *glow*?** We identify students who have mastered essential learning and provide extensions into deeper, more complex literacy experiences.

Source: Adapted from DuFour et al., 2016.

FIGURE I.2: The four critical questions of professional learning communities.

Integrating the beliefs and practices of the three big ideas and the four critical questions outlined in figure I.2 (page 9), Richard DuFour and his colleagues (2016) distinguished elements of a PLC that must be *tight*, meaning they are nondiscretionary, while most other aspects can be *loose*, or left up to teams to decide. In chemistry, an element is "a substance that cannot be broken down into chemically simpler components" (Lower, n.d.), and likewise, these tight elements of the PLC process cannot be broken into a simpler menu of options but must be considered *binding*—chemistry pun intended.

We find these tight elements so crucial that we used them to develop an acronym—*TEAMS*—that you can see explained in figure I.3 and used to organize this book's chapters to guide you through each step of literacy teams' critical work in the PLC at Work process.

	Tight Element of a PLC	What the Element Means for Teaching Grades K–6 Reading in a PLC at Work
1 **T** TEAMS	*Teams take* collective responsibility and work interdependently.	Develop systems and structures to support effective collaboration and communication, build a culture of mutual accountability for high levels of learning for all students, and work interdependently to achieve shared literacy goals.
2 **E** ENSURE	*Ensure* a guaranteed and viable curriculum.	Determine essential reading standards and create learning targets and reading progressions to drive unit planning and pacing.
3 **A** ASSESS	*Assess* and monitor learning regularly with common formative assessments.	Create team-developed common formative assessments for essential reading standards, set goals with students to improve reading, and then reteach, regroup, and reassess reading proficiency.
4 **M** MEASURE	*Measure* evidence of effectiveness of individual and collective teacher practices.	Use reading data to celebrate student progress, and analyze data to improve individual and collective reading instructional practices as well as inform upcoming reading instruction.
5 **S** SUPPORT	*Support* systematically with targeted acceleration, interventions, and extensions to meet all students' needs.	Create a systematic plan to extend students who are already reading proficiently and provide additional time and targeted support for students who need it. Continuously communicate and monitor student reading progress to increase the intensity of reading intervention when necessary (increasing frequency or duration or changing the teacher-student ratio, for example).

FIGURE I.3: TEAMS use of the five tight elements of a PLC at Work.

Reading the middle column of figure I.3 from the top down summarizes how teams are to operate in order to improve reading outcomes.

Teams take collective responsibility and work interdependently to *ensure a* guaranteed and viable curriculum, *assess* and monitor learning regularly with common formative assessments, *measure* evidence of effectiveness of individual and collective teacher practices, and *support* systematically with targeted acceleration, interventions, and extensions to meet all students' needs.

Now that we have explored the components of both literacy and the PLC process, we will spend the rest of the book examining the tight elements of teaching reading in a PLC at Work, which form the TEAMS process.

Putting This Book to Work

This book is divided into five chapters based on the five tight elements that must be embraced in a PLC at Work (DuFour, 2016b). Each chapter will help teachers and teams gain knowledge, understanding, tools, and examples for how to use each of those elements to improve reading instruction. This book guides literacy educators to do the following.

- **Chapter 1:** Ensure all team members have tools to collaborate and work interdependently to support all students' needs in reading and achieve team reading SMART goals.

- **Chapter 2:** Determine essential standards that address the crucial components of reading, pace the learning with proficiency maps, and create learning targets and reading progressions to drive unit planning.

- **Chapter 3:** Create team-developed common formative assessments for essential reading standards, analyze student data, and set goals with students to improve reading.

- **Chapter 4:** Use reading data to celebrate student progress, and analyze data to improve individual and collective reading instructional practices as well as inform upcoming reading instruction.

- **Chapter 5:** Create a systematic intervention and extension plan, monitor individual student intervention progress, reassess, and communicate with all colleagues who impact student reading achievement.

While we recommend that readers read through the chapters sequentially to gain continuity of the process, we, too, are busy practitioners who often catch sight of a useful tool and want to know how to use it right away. We understand you may flip through these pages and want to jump to one specific element your team is grappling with, so we designed the tools to stand alone to support teams no matter where they are on their PLC journey.

In the following chapters, we take a foundational reading standard as well as a comprehension standard for both literary and informational genres through the process, so by the end of the book, teams will have a model for what this work might look like from beginning to end for one of their reading standards. To help create clarity and establish a common vocabulary, a feature called Word Study defines key terms and ideas. Each chapter concludes with reflection questions and suggested next steps in Get Going or Get Better, so no matter where teams are on the PLC journey or in their quest to become more literate about literacy, educators will take away an action to help improve practices and change reading outcomes for all learners. At the end of the book, the appendices provide all the team protocols and templates highlighted throughout the chapters.

CHAPTER 1

Teams Take Collective Responsibility and Work Interdependently

As busy practitioners, we sometimes grab a new professional book, skim the table of contents, skip the introduction, and dig into chapter 1. We understand that many of our readers are already practitioners of the PLC at Work process, yet our constant concern is teams that are anxious to jump to tools do not continuously invest in doing the hard work of deepening their understanding. Please go back and read the introduction. Trust us.

After reading the introduction, you will be in the right purpose-driven frame of mind to ask yourself the following questions before you head into this chapter: "In my current school, do adults make decisions based on what is best for students, or what is most comfortable for adults? Are all policies, practices, and procedures examined in light of their impact on learning?" (DuFour et al., 2016). We are asking you to deeply reflect on that and think of some recent examples of literacy practices to support your answer. Be honest with yourself. Reflection is a critical step in this process.

If schools are to embrace these shifts, then they must examine structures, tools, and resources to support the work. All the systems, structures, and ideas in this chapter support teams in creating a framework for the hard work of collaboratively ensuring all students reach grade-level or higher proficiency in reading. We educators collectively make the choice every day to believe that our students are capable of accomplishing great things, and we do not relent. True collaboration during the PLC process requires rigorous professional learning. We facilitate growth. We create access.

We work to eliminate barriers. And most importantly, we maintain high expectations for every student we serve, and together, we create systems of equally high supports.

Developing a collaborative culture in your school, if that does not already exist, takes a concerted effort. It means taking a hard look at the current reality in your school and on your team and asking if what you're currently doing is what is best for students. Or, is it simply what is familiar and comfortable for the adults in the building? Taking steps toward what is best for students means focusing on collective efficacy and literacy SMART goals, having a master schedule that supports literacy learning, and having critical tools in place to support literacy teams. This chapter also includes the reproducible "Get Going on Chapter 1: Teams Take Collective Responsibility and Work Interdependently" (page 34).

Before we get more specific about how teams take collective responsibility and embrace collaboration, use those reading teacher morphology skills and break apart the word *collaboration*. Consider the prefix *co-*, which means "mutual or joint"; the root word *labor*, meaning "work"; and the suffix *-ation*, meaning "action or process." Collaboration means not just that you get along but that you *jointly co-labor through a process* to get the work done and accomplish a goal. In fact, sometimes when teams of teachers get along really well and are social outside of school, you can have an even harder time truly collaborating when tough decisions need to be made. We teachers value friendships and don't want to hurt a friend's feelings. Other times, real collaboration is challenging because humans are complicated and ever changing, yet we have to be willing to be vulnerable and trust our colleagues and also confront them and hold them accountable when necessary. After all, if we are truly collaborating and working interdependently, we can't meet our goal if our teammates are not also working to meet that goal.

WORD STUDY

collaboration *noun* [kə-ˌla-bə-ˈrā-shən] To work jointly with others or together especially in an intellectual endeavor (Collaboration, n.d.)

team *noun* [teem] A number of persons associated together in work or activity (Team, n.d.)

Collective Teacher Efficacy Through Literacy SMART Goals

Tom Carroll (2009), president of the National Commission on Teaching and America's Future, explains that "quality teaching is not an individual accomplishment, it is the result of a collaborative culture that empowers teachers to team up to improve student learning beyond what any of them can achieve alone" (p. 13). Individual teachers may be proud when their students accomplish a learning goal, but the quality teaching and empowerment Carroll refers to happens when a team of teachers sets a team SMART goal for all students in the grade level and accomplishes more as a team than any individual teacher could have alone.

Collective Efficacy

Collective teacher efficacy is defined as the "collective self-perception that teachers in a given school make an educational difference to their students over and above the educational impact of their homes and communities" (Tschannen-Moran & Barr, 2004, p. 190). Research shows collective teacher efficacy is three times more powerful and predictive of student learning than socioeconomic status, parental involvement, or student motivation (Goddard, Hoy, & Hoy, 2004; Hattie, 2012). Literacy teams develop collective efficacy through the PLC process by building a deeper understanding of literacy instructional design, utilizing evidence to address problems of practice, and making adjustments that lead to increased student achievement.

Teams with high collective efficacy willingly focus on student struggles because team members believe they can effect positive change. They show persistence when trying new teaching approaches because they believe they can get better results. Teachers with high collective efficacy are change agents who identify problems and collaboratively work toward solutions. These high-performing teams don't waste time admiring problems; they seek to resolve them.

For example, one team that Paula worked with in Texas had taught students to annotate text, but when the team members looked at their data, they found that students' underlining and circling of information wasn't increasing their comprehension. The team decided to ask the question, "What if we tried another approach?" Through their collective inquiry, they learned that if students wrote simple notes in the text margins, it might lead to better outcomes. And it worked! Because of their success, in the months that followed, the team confidently embraced the question, "What if we tried another approach?" And while some ideas fell flat, they focused on effecting change when students struggled. Their collective learning led to more and more students reaching reading goals. Effective results build a team's confidence and strengthen a team's belief that no matter the obstacle, their work can effect positive change.

WORD STUDY

collective efficacy *noun* [kə-ˈlek-tiv ˈe-fi-kə-sē] The shared self-perception of a group or team's capacity to positively impact students' academic achievement (Collective efficacy, n.d.)

Does that describe your team? If we want all students to become strong readers and we now know collective teacher efficacy is one of the top factors that impact student achievement, then we must take an honest look in the mirror and ask ourselves how we are functioning as a team. Are you simply a group of people assigned the same grade level or content area who divide and conquer the work? Richard DuFour (2009) often asked people to define the word *team* and clarified that a group of people working together *is not* a team. What is missing in that definition, as well as what is missing in many schools, is a key word: *interdependently*. A team *is* a group of people working interdependently to achieve a common goal for which they are mutually accountable. As you set literacy goals and work interdependently to achieve goal after goal together, your team develops that important sense of collective teacher efficacy.

A first step in moving from having goals that individual teachers may set for "their students" to interdependently working toward "our students" is setting a SMART goal for the achievement of all students across a team of teachers.

SMART Goals

Many schools set improvement goals, but not many reap the benefit of having teams set explicit short-term and long-term literacy SMART goals. Anne E. Conzemius and Jan O'Neill (2014) are credited with conceiving of *SMART* for goals that meet the following criteria.

- **Strategic and specific:** The goals are connected to priorities that link to overall objectives and are well defined and targeted to clear outcomes.

- **Measurable:** The goals are able to be measured using an identified tool to know when the goals have been reached.

- **Attainable:** The goals are rigorous yet not impossible.

- **Results oriented:** The goals are focused on student learning, not on what teachers will do.

- **Time bound:** The goals include the date when a team will analyze the results and celebrate progress.

Moving from a group to a team with high collective teacher efficacy requires team members to examine their current reality and collaboratively set a team SMART goal. We recommend two types of goals: (1) a long-term goal that measures student achievement in reading proficiency by the end of the school year and (2) a short-term goal that measures student achievement toward proficiency of reading skills in a shorter unit. Both types must include the criteria of strategic, measurable, attainable, results oriented, and time bound. The goals may look something like figure 1.1.

Current Reality	Last year, 76% of our third-grade students met the proficiency standard on our end-of-year reading assessment.
Long-Term SMART Goal	By May of this year, we will increase the percentage of third-grade students meeting the proficiency standard on the end-of-year reading assessment to at least 83%. Of those students who do not meet the proficiency standard, 90% will increase their score by at least ten points over last year.
Short-Term SMART Goal	Unit one: By October 17, 85% of third graders will be able to ask and answer questions using evidence from a text to demonstrate understanding (RI.3.1) by scoring at least 80% on the team-developed common formative assessment.

Source for standard: National Governors Association Center for Best Practices (NGA) & Council of Chief State School Officers (CCSSO), 2010.

FIGURE 1.1: Sample SMART goals for a third-grade team.

SMART goals drive the work of literacy teams, so you'll see them referenced throughout the book as each layer of the process is explored. Chapter 2 (page 35) will support teams to create unit goals on essential learning and set action steps to ensure teams reach their shared goals. Chapters 3 (page 63) and 4 (page 95) will guide teams in how to effectively monitor progress toward literacy goal attainment and highlight the importance of intentional celebrations when goals are met.

We've established that all professionals who serve students as readers must work collectively through effective collaboration, and we've set the stage for teams to rally around shared SMART goals to ensure their collaborative work is intentional, focused, and monitored. Next, staff need a master schedule that supports literacy learning.

A Master Schedule That Supports Literacy Learning

One of the quickest ways to ignite heated debate, induce tears, and create mile-long lines outside the principal's office is to mention a change in the master schedule. It is the biggest system change. The structure of a supportive master schedule that has time in the contractual day for teacher team collaboration *and* time for a systemwide response when students do and do not learn can be one of the greatest tools we have in ensuring all students learn at high levels. Some schools may need to revisit or refine their schedule, while some may need their leadership team to re-create whole systems in order to support their literacy goals. It can get a bit tricky, but it *is* doable. How does one even start this unnerving, complicated conversation? Collaboratively! Leadership teams work with teacher teams to create an effective schedule that prioritizes learning and collaboration.

First, look at a case study from our experience; then consider possible scenarios in yours.

Case Study

At one of our former campuses that is now a Model PLC, we knew that we needed as many heads, hearts, and hands around the master schedule restructuring as possible. We wanted to erase the idea that only administrators or those heavily invested in the master schedule (such as music or gym teachers, who serve every student in the building and often more than one class at a time) had a voice in how we would transform the time everyone spends at school.

First, we shared our driving purpose for transforming our literacy practices to ensure better reading outcomes for students and explained that to make that happen, we would have to challenge current structures. We weren't asking *if* the schedule should be changed; we were asking *how*. Then we asked our leadership team (composed of administrators, a counselor, instructional coaches, a special services teacher, and representatives from each grade level) to come together and brainstorm ideas. We took these ideas and brought a very rough first draft to the faculty.

Teachers shared some valid concerns we had to work through. For example, almost every grade level preferred to have literacy instruction take place in the morning, when students are fresh and ready to learn. Recess became another sticking point because most preferred recess blocks at the end of the day to maximize instructional time and limit interruptions. We had established consensus that we wanted the master schedule to support a system of interventions and extensions that made the most of our interventionists' and special services faculty's availability. This meant the literacy blocks needed to be staggered throughout the day so those team members could support each grade level during the crucial time that students were learning to read. Kindergarten and first-grade teachers had shared their collective experiences and provided anecdotal evidence that our littlest scholars tired out by the end of the day. They would have more difficulty producing writing or persevering when learning challenging new skills in reading at the end of the day than the older students, who have built up more stamina for a school day. So we agreed the master schedule would have reading blocks for the youngest students in the morning, the middle grades after lunch, and the oldest students last. The fifth- and sixth-grade teachers agreed and supported the decision even though they had to abandon their personal preference. We started to see true collective responsibility emerge for making decisions based on what is best for all students. By the time we presented the final draft of our schedule, all members of our staff had collectively agreed that this new schedule was fair, effective, and doable.

Considerations

Teams that are refining their master schedule might need to consider some additional situations that can make effective collaboration challenging.

- Some elementary schools have a team of two teachers who are departmentalized with only one person teaching literacy to both classes, so grade-level collaboration around grade-level literacy won't work. How do such teams flexibly regroup for collaboration and vertical teaming with teachers of like content in consecutive grade levels?

- On campuses with multilingual programs, the bilingual or dual language teachers can feel isolated because even though the learning outcomes are similar, the language of learning can make collaboration complicated. These teachers will need time with vertical teaming for collaboration around bilingual and multilingual essential outcomes in addition to grade-level and content collaboration for aligning essential outcomes regardless of the language of instruction. For one team in Virginia, a dual language teacher found it difficult to find text written in Vietnamese that aligned with the text written in English. This meant the team had to adjust texts frequently to ensure all students were engaged in the same text complexity regardless of language. That was a challenge in the limited time the team members had for collaboration. For another team in Texas, the kindergarten bilingual teacher's Spanish phonemic continuum didn't align with the English language phonemic continuum, making it complicated to compare proficiency levels as a team and then determine next steps for students who needed additional support. Both the teachers involved in these scenarios would have benefited greatly from vertical collaboration with other dual language and bilingual teachers on their campus or across the district to have time to build their expertise around the unique outcomes of their programs.

- Some specialized support teachers support multiple grade levels, which can make collaboration more challenging. How will teacher teams include their extended group of colleagues, such as special education teachers, interventionists, specialists, and paraprofessionals, in their collaborative team structures? These practitioners have insights, knowledge, and practices that are tremendous contributions in increasing students' reading achievement. Often, literacy support professionals are overlooked or excused from the collaborative process. Why would teacher teams exclude the educators responsible for the most vulnerable students from the most powerful system of support in education? Any educator responsible for ensuring students learn grade-level literacy essentials should be part of the collaboration. In our experience, this exclusion is often an oversight or a misunderstanding of who is part of the collaborative team. Ensure that all team members are present for as much of the collaborative team meeting as possible. If it isn't possible for every team member to physically attend collaborative meetings, create shared communication tools to ensure your work is accessible. (See the Shared Folders section for more about this topic on page 32.)

We are often asked to provide examples of master schedules for schools to duplicate when they are trying to prioritize literacy instruction. If only we could publish a one-size-fits-most template! We want to caution that there hasn't been a master schedule developed to date that will universally meet the needs of every campus. There are just so many considerations unique to each campus— number of students and faculty, instructional minutes, program and curriculum considerations, special services requirements, before- and after-school duty rosters, and more—that creating a viable master schedule for all schools is impossible. Plus, as you can see from our personal story, the staff have to own the decisions, productive struggle, and process that lead to the schedule that works best for their school. While it is a challenge to embrace the shared leadership of many stakeholders (rather than a few decision makers) contributing to the master schedule, the examples in figures 1.2 (page 20) and 1.3 (page 21) could be great starting points for team discussion that not only leads to a better schedule but also builds collective responsibility in the process.

Time	K	1	2	3	4	5
9:05	Morning Meeting	Morning Meeting	Morning Meeting	Morning Meeting	Morning Meeting	Morning Meeting
9:15	Reading	Science / Social Studies		Reading	Writing	Specials
9:25						
9:30			Mathematics			
9:45						
9:55						
10:00		Reading				
10:15					Specials	Mathematics
10:25						
10:35				Writing		
10:45						
10:50	Writing					
11:00			Lunch			
11:15	Recess	Lunch		Specials	Mathematics	
11:25						
11:30			Recess			
11:35						
11:45	Lunch	Recess				
11:55						Lunch
12:00			Writing and Word Study			
12:15	Quiet Time	Transition		Lunch		
12:25						Recess
12:40						
12:45						
12:50						

Source: ©2023 Mason Crest Elementary School. Adapted with permission.

FIGURE 1.2: First example of elementary school master schedule.

Time	Grade 4 English Language Arts/ Social Studies	Grade 4 Mathematics/ Science	Grade 3 English Language Arts/ Social Studies	Grade 3 Mathematics/ Science	Grade 2	Grade 1	K	Specials	Intervention
8:30–8:39	ELA 35 minutes	Mathematics 35 minutes	Social Studies 5 minutes	Science 5 minutes	ELA 5 minutes	Mathematics 60 minutes	Calendar (ELA/ Mathematics) 15 minutes	Grade 2	Grade 3 Intervention
8:39–8:45			Grade 3 Intervention	Grade 3 Intervention	Specials or Conference				
8:45–8:50									
8:50–8:55									
8:55–9:00							ELA 55 minutes		
9:00–9:05									
9:05–9:10									
9:10–9:15									
9:15–9:20	Grade 4 Intervention	Grade 4 Intervention	Integrated Social Studies 30 minutes	Science 30 minutes		Specials or Conference			Grade 4 Intervention
9:20–9:25									
9:25–9:30									
9:30–9:35					ELA 50 minutes				
9:35–9:40									
9:40–9:45									
9:45–9:50	ELA 60 minutes	Mathematics 60 minutes	ELA 95 minutes	Mathematics 95 minutes			K ELA Intervention	Grade 1	K ELA Intervention
9:50–9:55									
9:55–10:00									
10:00–10:05									
10:05–10:10									
10:10–10:15									
10:15–10:20									
10:20–10:25					Grade 2 ELA Intervention		ELA 25–40 minutes		

continued ▶

FIGURE 1.3: Second example of elementary school master schedule.

Time	Grade 4 English Language Arts/ Social Studies	Grade 4 Mathematics/ Science	Grade 3 English Language Arts/ Social Studies	Grade 3 Mathematics/ Science	Grade 2	Grade 1	K	Specials	Intervention
10:25–10:30									
10:30–10:35						ELA 30 minutes			Grade 2 ELA Intervention
10:35–10:40								Flex Collaboration Time	
10:40–10:45									
10:45–10:50	Integrated Social Studies 35 minutes	Science 35 minutes					Lunch		
10:50–10:55									
10:55–11:00					ELA 10–20 minutes				Grade 1 Mathematics Intervention
11:00–11:05					Lunch	Grade 1 Mathematics Intervention			
11:05–11:10									
11:10–11:15									
11:15–11:20									
11:20–11:25									
11:25–11:30	Specials or Conference	Specials or Conference	ELA 0–15 minutes	Mathematics 0–15 minutes			Recess	Grade 4	Conference
11:30–11:35			Lunch	Lunch		ELA 15–30 minutes			
11:35–11:40									
11:40–11:45									
11:45–11:50					Recess	Lunch			
11:50–11:55							ELA 25–40 minutes		
11:55–12:00					ELA 40–50 minutes				
12:00–12:05									
12:05–12:10			Recess	Recess					
12:10–12:15							Integrated Social Studies 30 minutes		
12:15–12:20	ELA 5–20 minutes	Mathematics 5–20 minutes	ELA 85–100 minutes	Mathematics 85–100 minutes					
12:20–12:25	Lunch	Lunch						Specials Lunch	Intervention Lunch
12:25–12:30									

Time	Grade 4 English Language Arts/ Social Studies	Grade 4 Mathematics/ Science	Grade 3 English Language Arts/ Social Studies	Grade 3 Mathematics/ Science	Grade 2	Grade 1	K	Specials	Intervention
12:30–12:35						Recess			
12:35–12:40									
12:40–12:45									
12:45–12:50					Grade 2 Mathematics Intervention		Specials or Conference	K	Grade 2 Mathematics Intervention
12:50–12:55						ELA 30–45 minutes			
12:55–1:00									
1:00–1:05									
1:05–1:10	Recess								
1:10–1:15									
1:15–1:20		Recess				Grade 1 ELA Intervention			Grade 1 ELA Intervention
1:20–1:25					ELA 15 minutes				
1:25–1:30	ELA 80–95 minutes				Integrated Social Studies 40 minutes		Mathematics 60 minutes		
1:30–1:35		Mathematics 80–95 minutes						Flex Collaboration Time	
1:35–1:40			Grade 3 Intervention	Grade 3 Intervention		ELA 40 minutes			
1:40–1:45									
1:45–1:50									
1:50–1:55					Mathematics 60 minutes				Grade 3 Intervention
1:55–2:00						Integrated Social Studies 40 minutes			
2:00–2:05									
2:05–2:10			Social Studies 5 minutes	Science 5 minutes					
2:10–2:15									
2:15–2:20									
2:20–2:25									
2:25–2:30									

continued ▶

Time	Grade 4 English Language Arts/ Social Studies	Grade 4 Mathematics/ Science	Grade 3 English Language Arts/ Social Studies	Grade 3 Mathematics/ Science	Grade 2	Grade 1	K	Specials	Intervention
2:30–2:35			Specials or Conference	Specials or Conference				Grade 3	
2:35–2:40							K Mathematics Intervention		K Mathematics Intervention
2:40–2:45									
2:45–2:50	Integrated Social Studies 30 minutes	Science 30 minutes							
2:50–2:55									
2:55–3:00									
3:00–3:05					Science 40 minutes				
3:05–3:10						Science 40 minutes	Science and Integrated Social Studies 45 minutes		
3:10–3:15			Integrated Social Studies 30 minutes	Science 30 minutes					
3:15–3:20	Grade 4 Intervention	Grade 4 Intervention							Grade 4 Intervention
3:20–3:25								Instructional Support	
3:25–3:30									
3:30–3:35									
3:35–3:40									
3:40–3:45									
3:45–3:50									

Source: ©2023 Tomball Elementary School. Adapted with permission.

Critical Tools for Literacy Teams

After there is a master schedule that emphasizes learning and collaboration, teams must determine whether they have the tools necessary to make that time as productive as possible. Some teams may already have norms, agendas, and shared folders, but consider how well your team uses those tools to help you collaborate around literacy goals.

Norms

Your work is complex, especially as teachers of reading, so having the right tools in place to navigate the tricky parts of becoming an interdependent team is critical. High-functioning teams are the engine that drives the PLC at Work process, which requires setting norms as guidelines and guardrails to shape collective behaviors (DuFour et al., 2016). Teams can start by clearly defining their norms. We know, we know. You might be rolling your eyes and considering skipping this section. Please don't! Norms aren't just for grumpy, dysfunctional teams. They are often overlooked or dismissed as unnecessary, but they are a key component of effective teaming. *Norms* are the behaviors we collectively commit to in order to collaborate productively, purposefully, and professionally (DuFour et al., 2016).

There is a difference between having norms and using norms. Rather than just coming up with a list at the beginning of the school year, consider always putting your norms at the end of your agenda and using the last minute of team meetings as a quick self-assessment. Questions like, *How'd we do holding each other mutually accountable for our norms?* or *What behaviors were helpful to our work?* can help teams determine if adjustments or recommitments to the expectations are required.

We advise teams to create a protocol that serves as a verbal or visual reminder to get back on track when a norm is broken. This can be as simple as invoking the term *reset* or a hand motion that indicates to each team member to self-check and correct. The clearer your team can be about how you all define and describe your expectations of each other, the more likely you will be to meet those expectations and function as a high-performing team. We highlight a few effective norms that teams have developed in the agenda examples provided in the next section. Additionally, in chapter 4 (page 95), we provide a script of an effective team meeting that shares how the team members hold one another accountable for team expectations.

Agendas

Just as norms guide behaviors, agendas guide outcomes (DuFour et al., 2016). Having an agenda focused on the tight elements of the PLC at Work process ensures the literacy team is collaborating on the right work. Basically, if a topic doesn't directly address one of the five tight elements of a PLC or answer one of the four critical questions of learning, it does not get invited into protected collaborative team time. A good agenda is more than just a list of items or compliance tasks to accomplish during collaborative team time.

If teams use agendas as just to-do lists instead of as ways to document the teams' work to revisit and refine as they continue to build shared expertise, they will likely be unable to remember their discussions and shared learning the following year. Having notes to reference each year helps teams access their thinking so they can pick up where they left off. A literacy team's work includes both process goals (such as developing effective strategies to build team consensus) and product goals (such as creating a focused common formative assessment with clearly defined success criteria).

Figure 1.4 shows a blank template for an agenda we created that can help teams stay focused on the right work. We designated spots for team norms and the critical questions of learning. There are also areas for notes and follow-up action steps so team members not able to join the meeting (such as interventionists or resource teachers who work with multiple grades) can stay informed. Additionally, there is space on the agenda for teams to allot specific amounts of time appropriate to the tasks or items. This paces out the work in a manageable way and helps keep the team focused. We have also included a place for teams to name and claim the celebrations of their work including reaching goals and gains in student achievement.

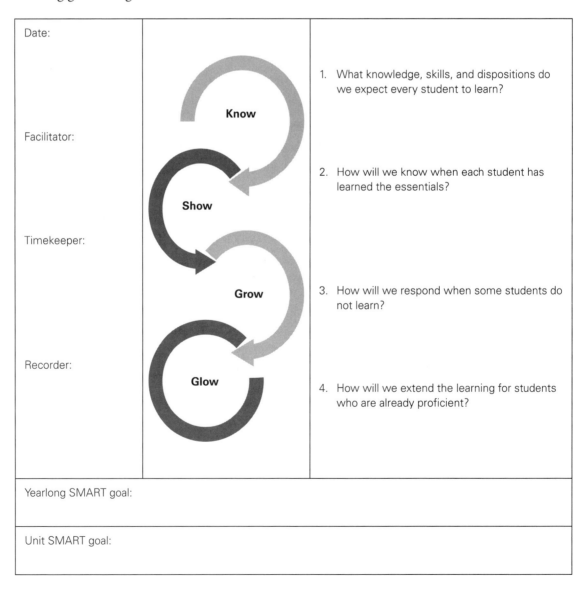

Date:		1. What knowledge, skills, and dispositions do we expect every student to learn?
Facilitator:	**Know**	
	Show	2. How will we know when each student has learned the essentials?
Timekeeper:	**Grow**	3. How will we respond when some students do not learn?
Recorder:	**Glow**	4. How will we extend the learning for students who are already proficient?

| Yearlong SMART goal: |
| Unit SMART goal: |

Topic and Time Allotted	Discussion Notes	Outcomes	Next Steps

Celebrations	Reflection on Norms	Tasks for Next Meeting Agenda	

FIGURE 1.4: Example agenda template.

The true challenge, however, isn't finding an agenda template that works for your team; it is filling it with only those agenda items that will have the greatest impact on student reading achievement so your collaborative time is well spent. The template in figure 1.5 (page 28) uses our TEAMS acronym for the tight elements to organize a menu of effective actions that literacy teams might choose from as they build a doable and productive collaborative team meeting agenda. Teams can use the agenda formatively to reflect on how effectively they used their time and determine what adjustments they need to make. In the following chapters, we explain more about how teams do these tasks, but as you scan the figure, think about the impact it would have both on

> The true challenge . . . isn't finding an agenda template that works for your team; it is filling it with only those agenda items that will have the greatest impact on student reading achievement so your collaborative time is well spent.

your students' reading achievement *and* on your individual and collective practices if your team focused on this work.

Literacy Team Tasks and Actions	Outcomes, Products, and Artifacts
T: Teams take collective responsibility and work interdependently.	
Goals	Develop team SMART goals for literacy.
	Develop short-term literary genre or unit goals.
	Set action steps for literacy goal attainment.
	Monitor progress toward literacy goal attainment.
Collaboration and communication	Develop, refine, or reflect on team-created norms and protocols to hold each other accountable and guide professional behaviors.
	Establish protocols for sharing information and providing access to all members of the grade-level, content, and support team.
	Organize literacy resources, products, tools, and templates into shared folders.
E: Ensure a guaranteed and viable curriculum.	
Identification and study of essentials for literacy	Review standards to align with state or provincial and local literacy curriculum.
	Identify essential literacy standards considering all critical components of reading.
	Study essential standards through published assessment examples.
	Ensure vertical alignment by grade level for continuity of standards and learning progressions.
Proficiency mapping and pacing	Pace the learning by essential literacy standards and learning target progressions.
	Align with the published scope and sequence or required reading curriculum or resources.
	Plan and pace feedback opportunities and classroom and team common formative assessments on a unit map.
Learning progressions	Unwrap essential literacy standards and create learning target progressions.
	Analyze and choose text for appropriate complexity and alignment with grade-level expectations.
A: Assess and monitor student reading achievement with ongoing assessment.	
Common formative assessments	Study reading assessment examples, question sets, and item banks released from test publishers.
	Create or curate team common formative assessments for each reading learning target.
	Create a common unit or summative assessment for essential standards in a literacy unit or genre study.
	Choose texts for assessments that align with the appropriate complexity and grade-level rigor.
	Decide as a team how students will access the texts.

Success criteria rubrics and proficiency	Determine proficiency levels for each essential reading standard.
	Develop success criteria and calibrate feedback and scoring.
	Create student data-tracking protocols and student self-assessment tools.
Work samples and exemplars	Create mentor texts (work samples) or exemplars for reading response.
	Analyze reading work samples to determine student proficiency and instructional needs.

M: Measure effectiveness of individual and collective teacher practices.	
Data study	Analyze common formative or unit assessment data results by essential standard and specific learning targets.
	Align reading assessment results with calibrated success criteria or exemplars.
	Set goals for reteaching and share and celebrate goals with students.
Decisions for practice	Determine collective team strengths and team opportunities for growth in literacy teaching and learning outcomes.
	Determine individual teachers' strengths and opportunities for growth in literacy teaching and learning outcomes.
	Include all collaborative support teachers in data study to improve or refine professional practices.
	Determine what additional supports, tools, or resources are needed for the team and individual teachers to improve teaching and learning in literacy.
	Align data outcomes with literacy SMART, team, or unit goal attainment.
Strategies shared	Build shared reading knowledge through embedded professional learning.
	Share best practices, tools, strategies, and resources in literacy.

S: Support systematically with targeted acceleration, interventions, and extensions.	
Intervention and extension groups	Create focused interventions for students who did not reach mastery of essential literacy learning targets.
	Create focused extensions for students who already achieved mastery of essential literacy learning targets.
	Group students for additional intervention or extension support by essential literacy learning target.
	Determine appropriate text complexity for intervention and extension.
Progress monitoring	Create and complete progress-monitoring tools for shared data collection.
	Create progress-monitoring tools for individual student data tracking and reflection.
	Clarify how those on the team leading interventions communicate with students' classroom teachers about progress so that learning transfers back to the classroom.

Source: Adapted from Kramer & Schuhl, 2017.

FIGURE 1.5: TEAMS tasks.

Teams do not attempt to accomplish all the tasks in this figure in one team meeting, but rather focus on different sections depending on where they are in their unit, cycling through most team tasks by the end of each unit. It is important for teams to think about what they need to accomplish unit by unit and break the tasks into chunks of work along the way. For example, figure 1.6 shows a weekly team agenda from Coleman Elementary School so you can see how the fourth-grade literacy team focused on specific tasks from figure 1.5 (page 28) while getting ready to begin a new unit on a nonfiction essential standard. It's a comprehensive and focused agenda that met the unique team's current needs.

Team Wildcats: Achieving success for students—every student, every day, every opportunity

Critical Questions of Learning to Guide the Right Work	**Norms and Commitments**
• Question one: What do we expect students to learn? • Question two: How will we know when they've mastered learning? • Question three: What will we do when they don't learn? • Question four: What will we do when they reach mastery?	• Address a breach with "Reset" and "Thank you." • Put phones facedown and silence them. • Stay within the agenda. • Model being a learner. • Present questions instead of complaints. • Never blame students or determine their limitations.

Team SMART goal: By May, we will increase grade-level reading proficiency for all fourth-grade students by 25% as measured by the end-of-year assessment.

Agenda for the Week of October 26

Time	Item and Alignment	Team Task	Outcome and Notes (Links)
2 minutes	Collaborative team process and procedures	Agree to norms and agenda.	Consensus on collective commitments
20 minutes	Question one Nonfiction unit: RI.4.2, "Determine the main idea of a text and explain how it is supported by key details."	Finish standard study from 10/19. Build learning progression of learning targets. Map learning targets for Tier 1 instruction.	RI.4.2 main idea template Nonfiction learning ladder Assessment examples Text examples

30 minutes	Question two Create common formative assessment for RI.4.2, "Determine the main idea of a text and explain how it is supported by key details."	Create classroom checkpoint. Create common formative assessment. Match text complexity. Begin success criteria rubric.	RI.4.2 main idea common formative assessment Classroom checkpoints and exit tickets
8 minutes	Collaborative team process and procedures	Bring completed exemplar for nonfiction open-ended response. Bring intervention and extension strategies for main idea. Share suggested short nonfiction text to use in small-group instruction.	Celebrations: Student growth increased by 8% on fiction unit assessment; intervention group progress monitoring was up by 15% on character analysis; Mrs. R's class has 100% attendance for virtual learning!
Parking lot: Virtual students locked out of form; return surveys to Mrs. Merrit.			
Questions that need answered: How will we rework the schedule to accommodate students recently identified as eligible for dyslexia intervention?			

Source for standard: Arkansas Department of Education, n.d.
Source: ©2023 Coleman Elementary School. Adapted with permission.

FIGURE 1.6: Fourth-grade weekly team agenda.

So now that you have an idea of what makes a useful agenda, can you think of what *doesn't* belong in a literacy team's collaborative meeting agenda? Sometimes it is tempting to take advantage of a team of teachers gathered in one place for an uninterrupted amount of time and instead focus on new reading resources, book studies, literacy vendor product presentations, field trip planning, baby shower organization, team events like reading night and parent orientation, or stern reminders from the attendance clerk. While all of these have value and are sometimes necessary, they don't belong in collaborative team time. Reserve this meeting for the team to focus on the things that have the greatest impact on student learning.

We are often asked for advice on how to stay focused when so many people are constantly asking teachers for meetings. Our best advice? Be crystal clear on what is invited into collaborative team time, and guard it from distractions. To help you navigate the different types of meetings literacy teams will likely encounter, table 1.1 (page 32) clarifies the differences between the collaborative team meeting that focuses on literacy through the PLC at Work process and other meeting formats that may put demands on teachers' time.

TABLE 1.1: Types of Meeting Formats

Meeting	Description
Collaborative team meeting	Teacher teams work interdependently to ensure student learning and mastery of essential standards and expectations in literacy. Teams focus on the five TEAMS elements and four critical questions of the PLC at Work process during this dedicated collaborative time.
Grade-level team meeting	Teams share grade-level or campus information, plan team or campus events, review routines and procedures, and complete team clerical or compliance-based tasks. These meetings usually include all teachers in a specific grade level regardless of content.
Literacy planning	Teachers may share ideas, frameworks, strategies, pedagogy, resources, books, and texts to create differentiated lesson plans. This time focuses on what the individual teacher will use, say, and do through the lens of teaching and effective initial instruction. This is also where discussion and planning for nonessential reading and literacy standards may occur.
Professional learning	Teaching staff come together by team, campus, or district to improve professional practices in teaching, learning, literacy assessment, and classroom culture and management. Teachers may learn from shared resources, book studies, articles, videos, or virtual professional learning or from teachers, instructional coaches, or consultants leading content or program-based learning. This is also time for teacher- or team-developed professional learning such as faculty share, colleague observations, learning walks, and reflective teaching practices and protocols that build shared knowledge and increase collective teacher efficacy, in literacy's case, in reading instructional practices.
Resource and compliance training	Teachers and other staff engage in training for a multitude of topics such as technology, reading programs or platforms, assessment proctoring and administration, new literacy resources or instructional materials, clerical responsibilities, health and safety, and policies and procedures.
Student study, intervention, or eligibility meeting	Teachers meet with administrators and campuswide support professionals to determine a plan of action or eligibility for support services for students experiencing learning or behavioral difficulties. These meetings may also be compliance meetings or progress-monitoring checkpoints for reading intervention programs. Campuses also use this type of meeting format for 504 plan or individualized education program (IEP) eligibility planning and implementation discussions.

Shared Folders

Another critical systemwide structure is formal organization of the literacy team's resources. Getting organized early and often allows teachers and teams to focus on the most important work: ensuring every student reaches proficiency in reading. We've learned the hard way about the value of organizing and housing all the documents, artifacts, templates, protocols, and materials your team creates in a shared platform as teams work collaboratively. Capture the work in a way that is quickly and easily accessed to maximize efficiency during collaborative team meetings. This allows extended team members (such as resource teachers, who may not be present during collaborative planning time) to access agenda notes, preview assessments, and share resources with the team. It increases effectiveness in the following school years and eliminates the hassle of trying to find a file that no one remembers the title of or trying to determine whose computer housed one particular resource.

A shared drive allows teams to go back each year and revise and refine instead of redo and replace. Most teams accomplish this by using an electronic shared folder platform such as Google Drive, Google Classroom, or Microsoft Teams. Some campuses and districts use a more secure platform, such as an internal network shared drive.

Whatever the choice, the following are the important criteria for the shared folders.

- They are a collaborative format where teams can simultaneously access, edit, and retrieve files.

- They are simple for teams to use and navigate.

- The expectation is set that the work of the team belongs to everyone on the team and is always saved to the shared drive.

It may make sense to organize your folders in a way that aligns with the different team tasks you'll be tackling as you teach reading, as shown in figure 1.7.

T	E	A	M	S
Teams take collective responsibility.	Ensure a guaranteed and viable curriculum.	Assess and monitor learning.	Measure evidence of effectiveness.	Support systematic interventions and extensions.
SMART Goals	Unpacked Standards	Common Formative Assessments	Data Analysis	Intervention and Extension Planning
Instructional Resources	Pacing Guides and Unit Plans	Student Data	Professional Development	Student Progress Monitoring

FIGURE 1.7: Sample organization of team literacy tools and resources in shared electronic folders.

Get Going or Get Better

As you think about your systems and structures to support literacy teams in ensuring that all students are reading at high levels, what changes, refinements, or complete overhauls would help transform collaboration and communication practices on your campus? Use the reproducible "Get Going on Chapter 1: Teams Take Collective Responsibility and Work Interdependently" (page 34) as a reflection tool for the learning in chapter 1 to move forward in the collaborative work of literacy teams.

Get Going on Chapter 1:
Teams Take Collective Responsibility and Work Interdependently

> » Who is part of your core team? Who is on your extended team? Do each of those people have a voice in the tasks your team tackles when taking collective responsibility for reading?

> » How do you currently prioritize time for collaborating around student learning, protected blocks of reading instruction, and a system of interventions and extensions? What adjustments do you need to make? What are you waiting for?

> » Is your team not just *creating* norms, agendas, and shared electronic folders but actually *using* them to become more effective and efficient in increasing student learning?

> » What is your team's current SMART goal? If you have to look it up, it isn't driving your work, so how can you make sure each member of the team remembers, refers to, and reaches for your goals?

Getting Started?	Getting Better?
When starting out, beware of *collaboration lite* (DuFour et al., 2016). Just changing your master schedule to allow time for collaboration does not result in a professional learning community. In the business world, you often hear the mantra that *culture eats strategy for breakfast* (attributed to Peter Drucker in 2006, as cited in Walters, 2022), meaning you can't come in and implement a new strategy unless you've first done the hard work of changing the culture to accept it. In PLC terms, we often say *culture eats structure for breakfast* (Muhammad, 2014) because you've got to develop the collaborative culture and start to take collective responsibility for all students' learning in order for any structural changes to lead to effective collaboration.	As you get better at this, beware of the common pitfalls that can plague teams when they go from just working together to working interdependently with a laser-sharp focus on achieving their goal of improving student reading. If there is absence of trust, fear of conflict, lack of commitment, avoidance of accountability, or inattention to results (Lencioni, 2010), it is time to have a crucial conversation, revisit and revise those norms and accountability protocols, and collectively recommit to working in a way that ensures success for all, teachers and students.

References

DuFour, R., DuFour, R., Eaker, R., Many, T. W., & Mattos, M. (2016). *Learning by doing: A handbook for Professional Learning Communities at Work* (3rd ed.). Bloomington, IN: Solution Tree Press.

Lencioni, P. (2010). *The five dysfunctions of a team: A leadership fable* (20th anniversary ed.). San Francisco: Jossey-Bass.

Muhammad, A. (2014). *Solution Tree Summit on PLC at Work* [Keynote address]. Phoenix, AZ.

Walters, A. (2022, March 31). Culture still eats strategy for breakfast. *Industry Week.* Accessed at www.industryweek.com/leadership/corporate-culture/article/21237760/culture-still-eats-strategy -for-breakfast on November 17, 2022.

TEAMS — 1 TEAMS — 2 ENSURE — 3 ASSESS — 4 MEASURE — 5 SUPPORT

CHAPTER 2

Ensure a Guaranteed and Viable Curriculum

Educators know more now than they have ever known about what works and doesn't work in schools. So, with all the research available on the art and science of literacy teaching and learning, why aren't they moving the needle? We propose that the reason educators have stalled is largely because they are trying to do too much. We know it's counterintuitive to suggest focusing on teaching *less* so students will learn *more*, but what if teachers stopped trying to teach everything and got really great at the things that matter most?

In his landmark study of what works best in schools, Robert J. Marzano (2003) finds that "one of the most significant factors that impacts student achievement is that teachers commit to implementing a guaranteed and viable curriculum to ensure no matter who teaches a given class, the curriculum will address certain essential content." When we say *guaranteed*, it is the collective promise of equity teachers make to their students. The term *viable* makes this promise doable. There has to be enough time for effective teaching and mastery-level learning to occur. Kathleen Dempsey (2017) from McREL International further explains:

> A "guaranteed" curriculum is often defined as a mechanism through which all students have an equal opportunity (time and access) to learn rigorous content. This requires a schoolwide (or districtwide) agreement and common understanding of the essential content that *all* students need to know, understand, and be able to do. The word "all" needs emphasis; a guaranteed curriculum promotes equity, giving *all* children equal opportunity to learn essential content.

The *E* in TEAMS represents the three key terms of establishing a guaranteed and viable curriculum: (1) *ensure* (we guarantee outcomes), (2) *essential* (what matters most), and (3) *equity* (for every student we serve). If literacy teams collectively determine what essential knowledge, skills, and dispositions all students must know and be able to do as readers, then they will achieve greater literacy outcomes for their students. But do teams know how to determine what matters most?

In this chapter, we give you tools and understandings to help your team work hard and succeed by naming the critical components of reading, determining and prioritizing what is truly essential in the reading standards, pacing learning across the year with proficiency maps, and deconstructing and reconstructing essential literacy standards to create learning targets and reading progressions that show how to meet students where they are and move them toward reading proficiency. This chapter also includes the reproducible "Get Going on Chapter 2: Ensure a Guaranteed and Viable Curriculum" (page 61).

Critical Components of Reading

The first step to ensuring a guaranteed and viable curriculum is making sure that the majority of your literacy block is spent on the standards and skills that matter the most in building proficient readers. Consider each of the critical components of reading and how they are represented in figure 2.1. As you read through the sections, consider the questions posed in each section as a team. Visit **go.SolutionTree.com/literacy** for a free reproducible version of those questions.

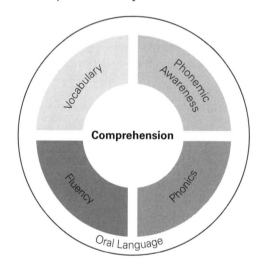

Source: Adapted from National Reading Panel, 2000.

FIGURE 2.1: Critical components of reading.

Comprehension, being the end goal or target of reading instruction, is the center pillar, surrounded by the other four of the National Reading Panel's (2000) five critical components—(1) phoenmic awareness, (2) phonics, (3) fluency, and (4) vocabulary. All those slices of the reading instructional pie are laid on a serving plate of oral language development. While oral language is not one of the five components of the National Reading Panel (2000) report, it is the foundation on which the other pillars are built.

As you begin to prioritize learning in the literacy block, you want to start with the importance of continuing to develop and expand students' oral language throughout the elementary years. Oral language development includes building a bank of known vocabulary words as well as understanding *syntax*, the rules that govern how words go together to form sentences, in spoken language. This development is key to becoming literate because students must draw on their oral language to transition from oral to written forms as readers and writers (Lonigan & Milburn, 2017).

Does your team provide opportunities for students to develop their *oral language* within the literacy block?

Vocabulary

When a word is not already in a reader's oral vocabulary, it will likely impede comprehension when it occurs in print, so we constantly build students' vocabulary through explicit instruction of definitions, implicit exposure to words, opportunities to encounter more words through reading, and graphic representations that make connections between what the students already know and new words they encounter. When students come across new vocabulary while reading, they check it against and link it to their oral vocabulary, which allows readers to decode unfamiliar words in print and translate them into speech that they can comprehend.

How will your team ensure students engage in tasks that expand their *vocabulary* during the literacy block?

Phonemic Awareness

This crucial skill of taking spoken words apart and putting them together is the foundation for learning to read. Phonemic awareness focuses on hearing and manipulating sounds, or *phonemes*, in spoken words. A heavy focus on phonemic awareness in the early years develops the ability to do the following.

- Isolate phonemes. ("Tell me the first sound in *pig*." /p/.)
- Identify phonemes. ("Tell me the sound that is the same in *ball* and *boy*." /b/.)
- Categorize phonemes. ("Which word does not belong: *cut, cup, bug*?" *Bug*.)
- Blend phonemes. ("What word is /s/k/i/p/?" *Skip*.)
- Segment phonemes. ("How many phonemes are there in *dog*?" Three: /d/, /o/, and /g/.)
- Delete phonemes. ("What is *school* without the /s/?" *Cool*.)

How will your team ensure early readers or those students who have difficulty decoding words develop strong *phonemic awareness* during the literacy block?

Phonics

Unlike phonemic awareness, which focuses only on sounds and can be done without ever looking at letters or print, phonics instruction focuses on attaching *phonemes* (sounds) to *graphemes* (letters) and using these letter-sound correspondences to read (decode) and spell (encode) words. As a result of phonics instruction, students learn to blend sounds in sequence to read new pseudowords, decode and encode regularly spelled real words, and eventually accurately and fluently read text containing both regularly and irregularly spelled words.

How does your team systematically build students' *phonics* skills and provide opportunities during the literacy block for students to apply those phonics skills to decode continuous text and encode to write for authentic purposes?

Fluency

Fluency is the ability to read text accurately at a conversational rate (similar to talking), with expression (*prosody*). To be fluent readers, students need well-developed phonics skills to decode accurately. However, word recognition skills alone do not necessarily lead to fluency, since some students may still read word by word rather than grouping words into phrases, or may read in a monotonous, robotic voice rather than changing inflection to show expression.

How does your team develop reading *fluency* during the literacy block so that students read accurately with expression, whether they are reading aloud or to themselves?

Comprehension

The ultimate goal of all reading instruction is comprehension. We read to understand. You saw in figure 2.1 (page 36) that comprehension does not get its own separate piece of the pie, but rather is the center of the graphic, surrounded by all the other components of reading that are needed in order for comprehension to happen. In their book *The Literacy Dictionary*, Theodore L. Harris and Richard E. Hodges (1995) define reading comprehension as "intentional thinking during which meaning is constructed through interaction between text and reader" (p. 39). Students develop comprehension skills as they become increasingly strategic with using background knowledge and strategies (making predictions, connections, comparisons, and inferences) to understand increasingly complex text.

How does your team ensure that all reading tasks lead to *comprehension* during the literacy block so students understand that the reason they develop their phonemic awareness, phonics, fluency, and vocabulary skills is so they can better read and understand any text?

Critical Components of Reading's Alignment With the Simple View of Reading

You may be familiar with a way to represent these critical components of reading through the Simple View of Reading (Gough & Tunmer, 1986), which breaks the component of reading comprehension into two parts: (1) word recognition and (2) language comprehension. Hollis Scarborough's (2001) Reading Rope then presents the Simple View of Reading in a graphic form to show how the strands included in word recognition and language comprehension interweave to produce fluent, skilled reading.

- Word recognition includes phonological awareness, decoding, and sight recognition.
- Language comprehension includes background knowledge, vocabulary, language structures, verbal reasoning, and literacy knowledge.

Figure 2.2 shows how the elements of Scarborough's Reading Rope hit the same targets as the National Reading Panel's pillars, represented earlier in figure 2.1 (page 36).

Simple View of Reading Components (Gough & Tunmer, 1986)	Strands of Scarborough's (2001) Reading Rope	Critical Components of Reading (National Reading Panel, 2000)
Word recognition	Decoding	Phonics
	Phonological awareness	Phonemic awareness
	Sight recognition	Fluency
Language comprehension	Vocabulary	Vocabulary
	Background knowledge Verbal reasoning Literacy knowledge Language structures	Comprehension

FIGURE 2.2: Alignment of reading components.

No matter your school, district, or individual pedagogy on the reading wars, you can assess your current reality to determine if reading instruction needs to shift to accommodate some missing or misaligned pieces of the critical components.

Essential Standards Determination

When teams start thinking about the entirety of all the teaching and learning expectations in literacy, their thoughts turn to not only those critical components of reading but also probably the many state, provincial, district, and federal guidelines that teachers are expected to teach. Through collaboration, you and your colleagues will drill down to team-determined essential standards. In some cases, you will have to work to clarify district-determined essential standards.

To provide some insights into how literacy teams have collectively embraced this work, we selected three reading standards from different standards documents that we think all readers will find useful. We will use these standards as examples in the coming chapters so you can see how the PLC process deepens teacher understanding as teams collaborate to unpack, pace, and create learning progressions, assessments, and unit plans for these standards. Table 2.1 shows the foundational reading, informational reading, and literary reading standards that will be used throughout the book. The foundational literacy standard focuses on phonological awareness, the informational reading standard focuses on comprehension of nonfiction texts, and the literary reading standard focuses on comprehension of fiction, drama, and poetry.

TABLE 2.1: Essential Standards Used as Examples Throughout This Book

Grade	Standard	Source
Grade 1	RF.1.3.E: "Decode regularly spelled one-syllable words that follow syllable types (closed syllable, open syllable, vowel-consonant-e, vowel teams, consonant-le, [and] r-controlled vowel)."	Foundational reading standard from the Arkansas English Language Arts Standards (Arkansas Department of Education, n.d.)
Grade 3	RI.3.2: "Determine the main idea of a text; recount the key details and explain how they support the main idea."	Informational text standard from the Common Core State Standards (National Governors Association Center for Best Practices [NGA] & Council of Chief State School Officers [CCSSO], 2010)
Grade 5	TEKS ELA.5.8.B: "Analyze the relationships of and conflicts among the characters."	Literary text standard from the Texas Essential Knowledge and Skills (TEKS; Texas Education Agency, n.d.)

Team-Determined Essential Standards

With all those literacy standards, how do literacy teams determine what is *essential* to produce proficient readers?

Let's start with what teams will need to gather as reference materials. We highly recommend the state or provincial standards for reading and districtwide guiding documents, such as a scope and sequence or pacing guide of suggested essentials. Additionally, many districts purchase reading curricula from various publishers, sometimes referred to as *scripted reading programs*. If that's the case at your school, teams must reference those suggested scope-and-sequence documents, too.

(Notice we said *suggested* because *teams* in a PLC—not the teachers' manual—determine what is essential.) Now that teams have curriculum tools and resources, where do they even begin?

As teams start to engage in the work of isolating standards as most essential, it can seem like an impossible task. There are so many layers of literacy standards, learning targets, skills, and dispositions, many of which are embedded and recursive as students progress through the literacy continuum. *Embedded and recursive literacy standards* are the skills, concepts, and strategies that continuously show up *because* you are reading, regardless of *what* you are reading, and they progress in rigor as the texts you read become more complex.

Some refer to this category of standards as *process* or *practice standards*. For example, determining word meaning in grade-level text is a skill that all readers work to develop every time they engage with text. Another example includes readers inferring meaning in text and citing evidence to support their thinking. While teams may introduce these standards and skills in isolation, these standards are meant to be a constant presence in the teaching and learning reading cycle.

WORD STUDY

> **embedded** *adjective* [im-ˈbe-dəd] Incorporated into something as an essential characteristic (Embedded, n.d.)
> **recursive** *adjective* [ri-ˈkər-siv] Returning again and again to a point or points already made (Recursive, n.d.)

With so much that students must master and apply to reach reading proficiency at or above grade level, how is it possible to narrow the scope of what is most essential?

Collaboratively.

Here are the general steps to this process.

1. Start with structured criteria that help determine what essentials teams will ensure with equity. (We recommend the R.E.A.L. criteria [Many & Horrell, 2014].)
2. Sort literacy standards into prioritized categories.
3. Reevaluate essential standards *at least* at the end of each unit and each year to help guide teams (as well as any other time data show a change in students' needs).

We highly recommend that literacy teams start with structured criteria that help determine what essentials they will ensure with equity. The R.E.A.L.—readiness, endurance, assessed, and leverage—criteria (Many & Horrell, 2014) have become the benchmark tool that collaborative teams turn to as a guide to select what matters most. With the scope of literacy standards, having a tool that helps teams identify and define the elements that make a standard essential is extremely helpful. Before Larry Ainsworth (2003) introduced the criteria of readiness, endurance, and leverage, and Tom Many and Ted Horrell (2014) added the assessment criterion to create the

R.E.A.L. acronym, teams had little support in deciphering what constituted a priority for learning. In figure 2.3, we share how we have applied the R.E.A.L. criteria to our work in literacy.

R: Readiness	Does it develop student readiness for the next level of literacy? Does it align vertically? Is it required for readers to become more strategic and advance in their reading or thinking?
E: Endurance	Will it last beyond this unit? Beyond this grade level? Is it valuable past a single text, genre, or assessment? Will readers engage in this skill or understanding as text becomes more complex?
A: Assessed or Accountable	Is it highly assessed at a mastery level? Are readers accountable to demonstrate continued understanding? Will readers monitor it as they work to become more independent in complex texts and tasks?
L: Leverage	Will it transfer across content and curricula when readers need to read in other subject areas and in life beyond school? Will readers be able to apply this thinking to understand text, tasks, and concepts more deeply regardless of the text type or application?

Source: Adapted from Ainsworth, 2003; Many & Horrell, 2014.

FIGURE 2.3: R.E.A.L. criteria for sorting what matters most.

As teams engage in conversations about which literacy outcomes are most essential, many teams struggle with how to classify standards that are important but don't exactly meet the R.E.A.L. criteria. Many teams ask, "If it's important but not essential, we feel like we have to address it; but what do we do with it?" Our response is always that we teach the important standards. And we teach them well. While we can guarantee that all students will be exposed to these important standards, we cannot collectively ensure that all students will master them.

To help organize the enormous scope of literacy skills and outcomes and focus the collaborative work of the PLC process, we encourage teams to sort literacy standards into three categories as suggested by Grant Wiggins and Jay McTighe (2005) in *Understanding by Design*. Each category represents a learning standard's importance level. We have adapted this framework and included descriptors to help teams distinguish among the three categories.

1. **Guaranteed:** The *essential* literacy standards, skills, and dispositions the team *collectively* guarantees all students will learn

2. **Engaged:** The *important* literacy standards, skills, and dispositions each teacher on the team *respectively* (the teacher individually) engages in with students through individual classroom instruction

3. **Introduced:** The *insignificant* literacy standards, skills, and dispositions they *selectively* introduce

We are frequently asked, "After teams establish essential literacy outcomes, how often should teams review the list for changes and updates?" Our answer is a pretty broad one: as often as required. We highly recommend reevaluating essential standards at the end of each unit and each year to help guide teams on whether they chose wisely. Revisit and refine the essentials as data indicate a shift in students' needs and an increase in the team's collective literacy achievement.

It is important to understand that utilizing the R.E.A.L. criteria or sorting standards into categories of *guaranteed*, *engaged*, and *introduced* is not meant to be a one-and-done checklist activity. It's an ongoing conversation. These tools and concepts are designed to guide the collaborative process of literacy teams. This is about productive engagement to build shared knowledge—not productivity alone.

As teams engage in this complex work, it's helpful to have a tool to anchor the thinking. We've included a simple tool to help teams chart reading standards by priority. Figure 2.4 shows a standards chart for a nonfiction reading unit from a fourth-grade literacy team in Tomball, Texas. We decided to share this team's artifact with generic descriptions of the standards for a more universal example. Remember, there is no universal list of what each team will guarantee as essential. This is just one team's determination of what to guarantee, engage, and introduce. Visit **go.SolutionTree.com/literacy** for a blank version your team can use to establish what is guaranteed, engaged, and introduced in reading. Literacy teams may also want to consider organizing identified essentials in a separate standards chart for each of the five components of reading.

Embedded and Recursive (*essential)	Essential and Guaranteed	Important and Engaged	Insignificant and Introduced When Appropriate
Infer meaning and cite text evidence to support thinking.*	Determine the main idea and explain how key details support the topic and purpose of text.	Provide a summary.	Identify and explain the author's use of anecdote.
Determine word meaning in text including figurative language.*	Analyze text structures in nonfiction text.	Utilize graphic sources to gain information from text.	Discuss how the author's use of tone and language contributes to voice.
Determine the purpose for reading.	Ask and answer questions in text to deepen understanding.	Determine the author's point of view.	—
Read multiple and increasingly complex texts fluently with appropriate rate,* accuracy,* and prosody.	—	Explain events, ideas, and concepts in text with specific information.	—

Source for standard: Texas Education Agency, n.d.
Source: ©2023 Tomball Elementary School. Adapted with permission.

FIGURE 2.4: Example of fourth-grade literacy team nonfiction reading standards chart.

*Visit **go.SolutionTree.com/literacy** for a free reproducible version of this figure.*

District-Determined Essential Standards

Some teams may assume that they do not have to engage in creating a guaranteed and viable curriculum because the district has already established a list of essential standards. Many districts do great work to determine a list of essential standards in literacy that will guide district-level pacing, curriculum resource alignment, and district-level assessments. Larger districts also seek to provide continuity to students who may move from one campus to another to ensure that no matter which campus they attend, there will be equitable outcomes. As Robert Eaker, Mike Hagadone, Janel Keating, and Meagan Rhoades (2021) lay out in *Leading PLCs at Work Districtwide: From Boardroom to Classroom*, "Every district must have a districtwide guaranteed and viable curriculum. A student's address should not determine what he or she is expected to learn" (p. 42).

However, if teacher teams are responsible for ensuring all students learn at high levels on what is deemed most essential, then teacher teams must be the professionals who lead the work. It is common for districts to invite teachers and instructional coaches to work on a committee and determine essential standards, pacing guidelines, and testing calendars. While teachers are *technically* at the table, grade-level teams are not. In this case, the work of the district committee is a great head start for teams, but the work doesn't stop there! Teams utilize the district list as a resource and guide to do the collaborative work of determining a list of essential literacy outcomes that meet the criteria of guaranteed and viable. The most important part of this process is for teams to build shared knowledge and expertise on what they will collectively guarantee all students will learn.

Here are possible steps for *teams* to take when district essentials have already been created.

1. Teams review each literacy essential on the list and determine alignment with the R.E.A.L. criteria (Ainsworth, 2003; Many & Horrell, 2014).

2. Teams review their current and historical literacy data to determine patterns of strengths and needs.

3. Teams study literacy assessment blueprints that outline how a summative assessment is designed, including item task analysis, example question stems, and frequency distribution of the assessed standards. They analyze vertical alignment and review literacy curriculum resources to help determine the viability of the number of essentials.

4. Teams may reduce the district's list to a few of the most critical literacy essentials to study as a collaborative team and guarantee for all students.

5. Teams move the remaining standards to the important engaged category (page 42) of literacy learning to ensure all students receive effective instruction in these identified standards.

Whether team clarified or team created, the work of identifying essential standards is a critical part of the collaborative work of teacher teams.

Proficiency Mapping to Pace the Learning

Once teams determine what is most essential, every shared decision made about instruction should *show* that these standards are prioritized and the focus of instructional time. Time for teaching and learning is your most precious commodity. There is never enough of it, and often, how you allocate time is guided by administration and district guidelines or published curricula.

In our work coaching literacy teams, we often find teams struggling to determine how to organize their time in the classroom to ensure that the teaching and learning of essentials is *viable*. In many cases, typical classroom literacy blocks include equal amounts of time for each literacy component. As we've noted, the emphasis on different components of reading needs to shift depending on where the teams' students are in the literacy continuum. While studying the National Reading Panel's (2000) recommendations for literacy and state and provincial reading standards, we began piecing together a better understanding of the types and scope of literacy skills that progress with each grade level. First-grade students need far more time engaged in learning to decode than in analyzing the purpose of text; sixth-grade students will spend more time inferring meaning through complex text than producing rhyming pairs to strengthen their phonological awareness (NGA & CCSSO, 2010; National Reading Panel, 2000; Texas Education Agency, n.d.).

By Grade Band

The visual representations built for kindergarten and first grade, second grade, and third through sixth grades in the following sections come from our experience in schools and can help teams map out the time needed to ensure mastery of essentials in correlation with each of the literacy components. Please note that the allotted time indicated in each slice is not a fixed and definitive final recommendation, but just one example of how Paula has helped teams work through spending their essential time wisely based on the volume of standards and the required levels of proficiency in each grade level.

KINDERGARTEN AND GRADE 1: SPENDING ESSENTIAL LITERACY TIME WISELY

Kindergarten and first-grade teachers spend a majority of their literacy block ensuring that all students reach grade-level proficiency in essential foundational reading skills such as phonemic awareness and phonics. These teams would identify a smaller number of essentials to guarantee in oral language development, shared reading comprehension, and written expression components. Proportionately, essential foundational literacy skills will become the focus for the majority of the time, as shown in figure 2.5 (page 46).

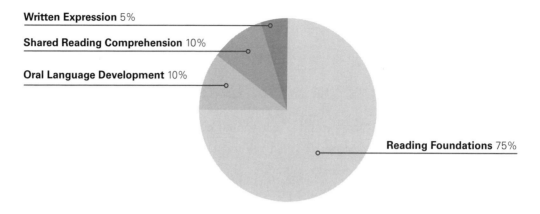

FIGURE 2.5: Example of managing literacy essentials in K–1.

GRADE 2: SPENDING ESSENTIAL LITERACY TIME WISELY

Second grade begins to transition students from proficiency in foundational reading skills to development of accountability for reading foundations (Paris & Hamilton, 2014). While essential standards in reading comprehension are still a critical component to ensuring all students reach grade-level proficiency in reading, teachers are able to decrease the amount of time spent on foundational literacy and spend more time ensuring students are mastering essential comprehension standards as required in increasingly complex text. Oral language development and written expression remain essential components, but teams determine the appropriate number of essential standards based on the unique needs of their students. An additional wedge of time is added for student mastery of language structures (grammar, syntax, and mechanics) in both speaking and writing. Proportionately, the number of identified essential phonological and phonemic awareness standards decreases while the number of essential reading comprehension standards increases, as shown in figure 2.6.

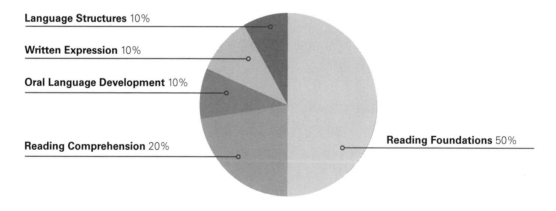

FIGURE 2.6: Example of managing literacy essentials in grade 2.

GRADES 3–6: SPENDING ESSENTIAL LITERACY TIME WISELY

In grades 3–6, students are now accountable for reading and understanding increasingly complex texts. Notice in figure 2.7 that the majority of time spent has flipped from foundational reading skills to reading comprehension.

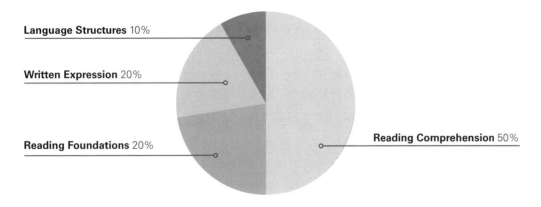

Language Structures 10%

Written Expression 20%

Reading Foundations 20%

Reading Comprehension 50%

FIGURE 2.7: Example of managing literacy essentials in grades 3–6.

Also note that foundational reading skills are still an essential component of reading in the upper elementary grades! The number of essentials in foundational literacy decreases, but foundational literacy's importance does not. Proportionately, teams identify more essential standards in reading comprehension, including the embedded and recursive reading competencies.

For the Academic Year

Once teams have allocated the minutes of the literacy block to align with essential outcomes, the next step is to begin pacing each essential standard in a year-at-a-glance format to map out the teaching and learning cycle. Many teachers already have pacing guides that are developed at the district level or are dictated by purchased curricula. These are good resources to use as guides and as starting points for your team discussion, but keep in mind only the teacher teams can truly *guarantee* that the literacy curriculum will be viable.

District or purchased curriculum maps lay out when to teach standards. But when a team builds a proficiency map, it shows not just when the team will teach the literacy essentials but at what specific pace the students will meet the grade-level expectation of each learning target. For example, texts found in curricular resources from publishers can include a laundry list of standards that are expected to be taught in a lesson timeline. Teachers will not realistically be able to ensure students reach grade-level proficiency in the essential reading standards in the publisher's suggested time frame or ensure students show consistent mastery of a reading standard or a skill in that standard in just one text. Teams need to adjust the publisher's scope and sequence based on the *team's* determination of when students are expected to meet the grade-level expectation for each essential standard. As well, not every standard taught in the curriculum in a given month, unit, genre study, or quarter warrants being on the proficiency map. This map is reserved exclusively for the essential literacy outcomes. The goal is to have a *one-page document* that makes it easy to see, at a glance, which standards you will assess and expect proficiency on each month, unit, or quarter.

Mapping learning outcomes can be tricky in literacy because of the many embedded and recursive reading standards that are integrated into most units. Some standards, such as determining the main idea or making inferences in text, appear multiple times throughout the year because you assess them on simpler text at the beginning of the year and continue to work through more complex text later in the year. Teams learn as they move through their proficiency maps that they might need to make slight adjustments throughout the year. Factors for adjustments might include data that indicate more time is needed in core instruction (due to a majority of students in the grade level not reaching proficiency) or unavoidable interruptions to instruction (such as school closures or a large number of unexpected absences). We recommend trying to stay as close to the team's pacing calendar as possible because borrowing time from one essential to ensure another can cause achievement gaps.

Figure 2.8 shows a sample proficiency map for third grade done by quarter. It includes the number of weeks in each quarter so teams can ensure their pacing matches the number of instructional days available to them. From the year-at-a-glance proficiency map, you can begin to see learning outcomes emerge by units or genre study.

Essential Standards Assessed	First Quarter Eight weeks	Second Quarter Nine weeks	Third Quarter Nine weeks	Fourth Quarter Ten weeks
Literary reading and informational texts	**Focus genre: Realistic fiction** RL.3.1: Answer text questions using evidence. RL.3.3: Describe character actions applied to events.	**Focus genre: Nonfiction** RI.3.2: Determine main idea and key details. RI.3.8: Describe text structure (time order).	**Focus genre: Fiction (including folktales and fables)** RL.3.2: Recount: formal written or oral ordering of narrative events. RL.3.1: Answer text questions using evidence.	**Focus genre: Nonfiction** RL.3.2: Determine theme from stories using key details. RI.3.8: Describe text structure (cause/effect). RI.3.9: Compare and contrast main idea and key details.
Oral language and reading foundations	RF.3.3c: Decode multisyllable words.	RF.3.3a: Identify and know the meaning of the most common prefixes and derivational suffixes.	RF.3.3c: Decode multisyllable words.	RF.3.4: Read grade-level text with sufficient accuracy and fluency to support comprehension.
Embedded and recursive standards	—	RF.3.4c: Use context clues in a sentence to determine meaning.	RF.3.4c: Use context clues in a sentence to determine meaning.	RI.3.10: Read grade-level informational text in different subject areas.

Source for standard: NGA & CCSSO, 2010.
Source: Adapted from Kramer & Schuhl, 2017.

FIGURE 2.8: Third-grade year-at-a-glance proficiency map by quarter.

TEAMS Process Protocol for Deconstructing Essential Standards

Critical question one of the PLC at Work process doesn't end with literacy teams identifying what all students must know and be able to do, allocating time to focus on the essentials, and pacing the proficiency in literacy outcomes throughout the year. These team decisions and guiding documents are the beginning of the complex work of building shared knowledge and clarity around the following three things in each of the essential literacy outcomes.

1. What learning looks like (evidence of students' learning)
2. What learning sounds like (students' use of academic language and discourse)
3. What learning feels like (students' sense of self-efficacy)

Standards aren't always written with clarity and might lead to different interpretations teacher by teacher. In this process, teams develop expertise on each step of stated, implied, or embedded learning in the essential standards. *We* must be students of the standards *before* we bring the standards to our students.

> *We* must be students of the standards *before* we bring the standards to our students.

The next step for teams is to identify the individual learning targets in each of the identified essential literacy standards and become experts in designing equitable outcomes through effective teaching and learning practices. Learning targets are small pieces of learning in the essential standard that help students understand exactly what it is they are learning, the level of complexity of their learning, and how they will show what they've learned (Moss, Brookhart, & Long, 2011). Learning targets provide a more precise answer to critical question one of the PLC process, "What is it we want our students to know and be able to do?" (DuFour et al., 2016, p. 59). For example, in the third-grade Common Core standard, "Determine the main idea of a text; recount the key details and explain how they support the main idea" (RI.3.2; NGA & CCSSO, 2010), there is more than one outcome readers must tackle. Within this essential standard, students must do the following three things.

1. Determine the main idea of a nonfiction text.
2. Recount the key details.
3. Explain how the key details support the main idea.

These reading skills build on each other to a more complex level of comprehension. Isolating each component helps literacy teams ensure they are designing with precision each step along the way.

Learning targets in essential reading standards represent the following criteria (Wiggins & McTighe, 2005).

- A precise amount of learning—a small piece of an essential reading standard
- Student-friendly language inclusive of essential academic vocabulary
- The expected level of thinking or complexity of text
- How students will demonstrate their learning
- Steps in the progression from least complex to most complex
- A clear pathway for students to reach mastery level of essential reading standards

Literacy teams deconstruct only essential reading standards into learning targets. This process can be daunting, so we developed a step-by-step protocol to help guide your team's collective discussions and collaborative learning around essential literacy standards. A word of caution: Compliance-driven outcomes are not the intention of this work. Teams must commit to, not comply with, the process. Please do not look at this tool as a checklist to complete. This tool is meant to be used as a discussion guide for teams to gain clarity and expertise on the essential literacy expectations that they will guarantee for all students. Some teams starting the process might need every step of this protocol, while seasoned teams might have a more organic process or find a few additional layers to add to their collective thinking.

A summary of the protocol follows.

- **Steps 1–4** ask teams to learn from the mentor texts and documents that provide insights on the intention of the literacy standard, the vertical alignment, and the cognitive rigor level of assessments. Teams don't always get what they need from the standard alone, so they have to analyze available resources to learn what the standard is actually asking students to know or be able to do.

- **Steps 5–7** ask teams to study the language of the standard. What level of thinking and reasoning are students accountable for? What vocabulary will they be expected to use to demonstrate their understanding? What behaviors will readers need to demonstrate? Teams also identify scaffolds, such as sentence frames, to support oral language development as students use key academic terms to communicate about their learning.

- **Steps 8–10** ask teams to construct learning targets that break the standard into small aligned goals that articulate what students must do for each phase of the learning. Additionally, teams construct coaching questions that guide students through productive struggle, and they group targets into logical chunks of learning. These targets become critical tools in the teaching, learning, and assessing cycle. As author Nicole Dimich (2015) states, "Teasing out the learning goals from standards creates the foundation for our instruction (lesson plans, activities), our assessments (both formative and summative), and our curriculum (the resources tapped to plan instruction and assessment)" (p. 27).

Here are the steps to the deconstructing essential standards protocol, which also appears in appendix A as the reproducible "TEAMS Process Protocol for Deconstructing Essential Standards" (page 138).

1. **Label** the unit by genre or focus, and list the essential standards that align with this unit. Then copy and paste the primary essential standard into the Essential Standard to Deconstruct box.

2. **Look** at the essential standard vertically. What can we learn about the standard in the grade level below us? Above us? What prerequisite skills will students need to access?

3. **Read** any explanations about the standard in the state or provincial standards document or other curriculum guides. Discuss and record understandings.

4. **Consider** what the team can learn from assessment blueprints or released assessment items.

5. **Pull** nouns and related vocabulary from the standard to list common language teachers will use in instruction and accountable language students will use to share their thinking and learning.

6. **Pull** verbs and related vocabulary from the standard to list skills or behaviors students will demonstrate to show their understanding.

7. **Generate** sentence frames or vocabulary stems around academic vocabulary.

8. **Use** the nouns and verbs list to build learning targets shared as *I can* statements, breaking the essential standard into bite-size pieces for student-friendly learning goals. Start with the simplest targets, and build to the more complex or difficult ones, ending with the overall grade-level task that puts all the pieces together.

9. **Create** questions to assist students in guiding their own thinking and to deepen understanding of each *I can* statement.

10. **Group** *I can* statements into related learning goals to guide instruction and informal assessment or feedback to put some of the smaller pieces together in a way that will make sense in the teaching and learning cycle. Use brackets or highlight in a different color for each grouping.

Figure 2.9 (page 52) is an example of how a first-grade team documented its shared discussion and thinking on an essential literacy standard using this protocol. See appendix B for the customizable reproducible "TEAMS Process Template: Deconstructing Essential Standards" (page 144).

1. **Label** unit: Fiction details All standards in this unit: Know and apply grade-level phonics and word analysis skills in decoding words. Read grade-level text with sufficient accuracy and fluency to support comprehension. Ask and answer questions about key details in a text. Describe characters, settings, and major events in a story, using key details.	Essential standard to deconstruct: RF.I.3.E: Decode regularly spelled one-syllable words that follow syllable types (closed syllable, open syllable, vowel-consonant-e, vowel teams, consonant-le, and r-controlled vowel).
2. **Look** at standard in grade level below: RF.K.3.E: Decode CVC words.	Standard in grade level above: RF.2.3.E: Decode words that follow the six syllable types (closed syllable, open syllable, vowel-consonant-e, vowel teams, r-controlled, consonant-le).

Prerequisite skills:

Know all consonant, short vowel, and long vowel sounds.

Blend sounds in sequence.

Produce the correct sound for blends and digraphs.

Correctly decode regularly spelled CVC, CCVC, and CVCC closed syllable words.

3. **Read** notes in local standards or other curriculum guides and record understandings:

» Closed syllable = A syllable with a short vowel spelled with a single vowel letter ending in one or more consonants

» Open syllable = A syllable that ends with a long vowel sound, spelled with a single vowel letter

» Vowel-consonant-e syllable = A syllable with a long vowel spelled with one vowel + one consonant + silent *e*

» Vowel team syllable = A syllable that uses two to four letters to spell the vowel

» R-controlled syllable = A syllable with *er, ir, or, ar,* or *ur* where vowel pronunciation often changes before /r/

» Consonant-le syllable = An unaccented final syllable containing a consonant before /l/ followed by a silent e

4. **Consider** understandings from assessment blueprints and released assessment items:

Must break multisyllable words into syllables and identify each type of syllable.

Need to be able to identify the type of syllable no matter what position it occurs within a word (first, second, third syllable).

Syllabication rules apply to nonsense words as well as real words.

5. **Pull** nouns or content in standard (plus related vocabulary):	6. **Pull** verbs or skills in standard (plus related vocabulary):
Syllable	Decode
Syllable types	Follow
Closed syllable	Related vocabulary:
Open syllable	» Blend
Vowel-consonant-e	» Identify
Vowel teams	
Consonant-le	
R-controlled vowel	
Related vocabulary:	
None	

7. **Generate** sentence frames or vocabulary stems around academic vocabulary:

Vowels make more than one sound.

This is a closed syllable, so I read it with a short vowel sound.

This is an open/vowel-consonant-e/vowel team syllable, so I read it with a long vowel sound.

This syllable has a bossy r that controls the vowel and makes it change its sound.

Where do I divide this word into syllables?

8. **Use** nouns and verbs to create student-friendly *I can* statements arranged in a learning progression from simple to complex:

I can identify and produce the short vowel sounds.

I can identify and produce the long vowel sounds.

I can identify and produce the r-controlled vowel sounds.

I can read closed syllables with short vowel sounds.

I can read open syllables with long vowel sounds.

I can read vowel-consonant-e syllables with long vowel sounds.

I can read vowel team syllables with long vowel sounds.

I can read words that end in a vowel-consonant-le syllable.

I can read r-controlled vowel syllables.

I can determine the syllable type of unknown words and apply what I know to read new words.

FIGURE 2.9: Deconstructing essential standards protocol—Foundational reading standard for first grade deconstructed.

continued ▶

9. **Create** guiding questions for *I can* statements:

I can identify and produce the short vowel sounds.
  » Which letter in this syllable is the vowel? Do I see an *a, e, i, o,* or *u*? What is my anchor word for that short vowel sound?

I can identify and produce the long vowel sounds.
  » Which letters in this syllable are the vowels? Is there a vowel team or a silent *e*? What is my anchor word for that long vowel sound? Does the vowel say its name?

I can identify and produce the r-controlled vowel sounds.
  » Is the vowel followed by an r? What is my anchor word for that r-controlled vowel sound?

I can read closed syllables with short vowel sounds.
  » Is there a consonant after the vowel closing it in? How does this syllable sound with a short vowel sound? Have I blended the sounds in sequence?

I can read open syllables with long vowel sounds.
  » Is the vowel the last letter in the syllable? How does this syllable sound with a long vowel sound? Have I blended the sounds in sequence?

I can read vowel-consonant-e syllables with long vowel sounds.
  » Is there an e at the end of the word? How does this syllable sound with a long vowel sound? Have I blended the sounds in sequence? Why is the e on the end of the word?

I can read vowel team syllables with long vowel sounds.
  » Are there two vowels next to each other? How does this syllable sound with a long vowel sound? Have I blended the sounds in sequence?

I can read words that end in a vowel-consonant-le syllable.
  » Does the syllable end in le?

I can read r-controlled vowel syllables.
  » Does an r follow the vowel? How does the bossy r make that vowel change its sound?

I can determine the syllable type of unknown words and apply what I know to read new words.
  » Is this syllable open or closed? Should I try a short vowel or long vowel sound? What do I notice about the vowel(s) in this syllable? How does the word end? Does that sound like a word I've heard before?

10. **Group** *I can* statements into related learning goals:

I can identify and produce the short vowel sounds.

I can identify and produce the long vowel sounds.

I can identify and produce the r-controlled vowel sounds.

_____

I can read closed syllables with short vowel sounds.

I can read open syllables with long vowel sounds.

_____

I can read vowel-consonant-e syllables with long vowel sounds.

I can read vowel team syllables with long vowel sounds.

_____

I can read words that end in a vowel-consonant-le syllable.

I can read r-controlled vowel syllables.

_____

I can determine the syllable type of unknown words and apply what I know to read new words.

Source for standards: Arkansas Department of Education, n.d.

Figure 2.10 is an example of how a fifth-grade team documented its shared discussion and thinking on an essential literacy standard using this protocol.

1. **Label** unit: Fiction literature All standards in this unit: » Compare and contrast two or more characters, settings, or events in a story or drama, drawing on specific details in the text (e.g., how characters interact). » Determine a theme of a story, drama, or poem from details in the text, including how characters in a story or drama respond to challenges. » Determine the meaning of words and phrases as they are used in a text, including figurative language. » Refer to details and examples in a text when explaining what the text says explicitly and when drawing inferences from the text. » Compare and contrast the treatment of similar themes and topics.	Essential standard to deconstruct: RL.5.3: Compare and contrast two or more characters, settings, or events in a story or drama, drawing on specific details in the text (e.g., how characters interact).
2. **Look** at standard in grade level below: RL.4.3: Describe in depth a character, setting, or event in a story or drama, drawing on specific details in the text (e.g., character's thoughts, words, or actions).	Standard in grade level above: RL.6.3: Describe how a story's or drama's plot unfolds in a series of events as well as how the characters respond or change as the plot moves toward a resolution.

Prerequisite skills:

Plot structure: characters, setting, problem, events, solution

Describe character or traits (actions, words, thoughts, and motivations).

Determine events of a story.

Vocabulary terms for character analysis

Some understanding of theme and connection to character lesson

Determine word meaning with emotion-focused figurative language.

3. **Read** notes in local standards or other curriculum guides and record understandings:

The shift is the comparison of two or more characters and inferring the relationships as they relate to the plot.

FIGURE 2.10: Deconstructing essential standards protocol—Essential reading comprehension standard for fifth grade deconstructed.

continued ▶

4. **Consider** understandings from assessment blueprints and released assessment items:

Conclude or infer about relationships and why characters interact.

Characters' thoughts, actions, and motivations drive many of the task and answer choices.

Focus of the story shifts or plot structure

Sorting characters based on outcomes and plot resolution

How does each character feel?

Text evidence required for all inferences; go back and reread.

Figurative language shows up in many question stems when it describes what a character thinks.

Perspective for point of view, but not from author's craft

---

5. **Pull** nouns or content in standard (plus related vocabulary):

Character, setting, events, specific details

Text, interact

Related vocabulary:

Depth, thoughts, words, actions, motivation

Drive, shift, focus, "best" choice or answer

Figurative language, infer, cite text evidence

Support, character actions, traits, dialogue

Internal versus external, perspective, compare

Contrast

6. **Pull** verbs or skills in standard (plus related vocabulary):

Compare, contrast

Related vocabulary:

Describe, draw, infer, determine, refer

Include, explain, cite, analyze

---

7. **Generate** sentence frames or vocabulary stems around academic vocabulary:

Citing text evidence is providing proof for your answer to a question.

The character did _____ and the passage states _____.

The character was motivated (the cause or reason why) to _____ because _____.

The actions of a character help the plot because _____.

Dialogue is showing a conversation between characters. They are talking back and forth.

Figurative language is using words in an interesting way. The author uses the words or phrase _____ to show _____.

We can infer the character is feeling _____ based on _____.

The character's motivation was . . .

Character A responded _____ when Character B did (or said) _____.

The problem could have been avoided if the character had _____.

8. **Use** nouns and verbs to create student-friendly *I can* statements arranged in a learning progression from simple to complex:

I can identify essential characters.

I can identify the problem.

I can identify the solution.

I can describe the major events in a story.

I can analyze characters' thoughts, actions, and motivations.

I can explain the actions and interactions of characters.

I can compare and contrast characters, ideas, and events within stories.

I can infer meaning in text.

I can cite evidence from text to support my thinking.

9. **Create** guiding questions for *I can* statements:

<u>I can identify essential characters.</u>

Does the character add to the problem or solution of the story? Would the character be missed if they weren't in the story? Would the story still make sense? Who has the main problem (protagonist)? Who is making the problem worse (antagonist)?

<u>I can identify the problem.</u>

What is the essential problem? The biggest obstacle to overcome? What's most important to the story? Which problem must be addressed in order for the story to continue or make sense?

<u>I can identify the solution.</u>

How does the story turn out for the main character (protagonist)? How is the problem resolved?

<u>I can describe the major events in a story.</u>

What events lead to the solution of the problem? What events caused the problem or made it worse? Which key details support the plot? What if this event weren't in the story? Would the story still make sense? Can I retell the major events in an order that makes sense?

<u>I can analyze characters' thoughts, actions, and motivations.</u>

What does the character say, think, or do? Why is the character speaking, thinking, or acting the way they do? What makes the character feel that way? How does the character make others feel? What is this character's point of view or perspective? What is this character's greatest challenge? Fear? Goal? Accomplishment?

<u>I can explain the actions and interactions of characters.</u>

How do the characters react to each other? What are the characters feeling toward each other? Why does the character respond to other characters in this way? What does the dialogue show about X? How would the story change without one of these characters? What's at stake?

<u>I can compare and contrast characters, ideas, and events within stories.</u>

How are these characters alike? How are they different? Why? How did each character react to the same situation? What traits or behaviors are similar?

<u>I can infer meaning in text.</u>

What is the author trying to say, but isn't? What background knowledge can I use? What clues can I use to connect the dots? What do I need to think about? How does this support the plot?

<u>I can cite evidence from text to support my thinking.</u>

What does the text say? Can I prove it? Can I back up my answer with text evidence? Can I quote from the text? What does the author say to support my thinking?

continued ▶

10. **Group** *I can* statements into related learning goals:

I can identify essential characters.

I can identify the problem.

I can identify the solution.

I can describe the major events in a story.

I can analyze characters' thoughts, actions, and motivations.

I can explain the actions and interactions of characters.

I can compare and contrast characters, ideas, and events within stories.

I can infer meaning in text.

I can cite evidence from text to support my thinking.

Source for standards: NGA & CCSSO, 2010.

Now that they've studied and deconstructed the standards down to the last detail, teams *reconstruct the standards into a learning progression and plan.

> When teams are able to articulate what learning must occur at each step in the learning progression, teachers are able to respond quickly and effectively when students do and do not learn.

While it may seem that we've exhausted the conversation about this essential literacy outcome, from here teams dive even deeper into the process of studying standards. To have teams develop the learning progression into a learning *plan*, we ask them to engage in another layer of building a guaranteed and viable curriculum. Since each learning target is a guaranteed outcome for all students, we ask teams to define with even greater depth and clarity the learning connected to each learning target. When teams are able to articulate what learning must occur at each step in the learning progression, teachers are able to respond quickly and effectively when students do and do not learn. We ask teams to apply the four critical questions of the PLC at Work process for each step of learning. For the work in reconstructing essential literacy standards, teams would discuss proven instructional strategies that would be most effective, types of appropriate text, and common misconceptions that teams can proactively address in the teaching and learning cycle.

Again, the collaborative process is the most important part of teams' work, so the following protocol is not a tool that is meant to be checked off like a to-do list. It is a document that guides the rich conversations and intentional learning of collaborative literacy teams. With this kind of clarity, teams are ready to implement effective teaching and learning practices to ensure all students reach grade-level proficiency or higher in essential literacy outcomes. Figure 2.11 shows a team's expanded thinking on an essential learning target from their work in deconstructing the standard's learning outcomes. See appendix B for the reproducible "Deconstructing and Reconstructing Essential Learning Targets: Critical Question One (Know)" (page 146).

Unit:			
Literary texts—fiction			

Essential Literacy Standard:

RL.5.3—Compare and contrast two or more characters, settings, or events in a story or drama, drawing on specific details in the text (e.g., how characters interact).

Learning Target		Question One: Know	Team Notes
I can identify essential characters.	→	Instructional strategies? Misconceptions? Appropriate text?	Graphic organizer (plot summary frame) Character list and explanation of why essential Listing all the characters—which are essential to the problem or solution? Under the Lemon Moon (Fine, 1999; entry text) The Watsons Go to Birmingham—1963 (Curtis, 2013; grade-level text)
I can identify the problem.	→	Instructional strategies? Misconceptions? Appropriate text?	Graphic organizer (plot summary frame) Cause-effect chart Listing any conflict or negative interaction Under the Lemon Moon (Fine, 1999; entry text) The Watsons Go to Birmingham—1963 (Curtis, 2013; grade-level text)
I can identify the solution.	→	Instructional strategies? Misconceptions? Appropriate text?	Graphic organizer (plot summary frame) Cause-effect chart Naming the conclusion of the story Under the Lemon Moon (Fine, 1999; entry text) The Watsons Go to Birmingham—1963 (Curtis, 2013; grade-level text)
I can describe the major events in a story.	→	Instructional strategies? Misconceptions? Appropriate text?	Action step / event graphic organizer / model Confusing ancillary events with major events that drive plot / too many details Enemy Pie (Munson, 2000; shared and modeled) The Watsons Go to Birmingham—1963 (Curtis, 2013; grade-level text)

FIGURE 2.11: Fifth-grade team example of deconstructing and reconstructing by learning target—Critical question one (know).

continued ▶

Learning Target		Question One: Know	Team Notes
I can analyze characters' thoughts, actions, and motivations.	➡	Instructional strategies? Misconceptions? Appropriate text?	Connecting dialogue and actions to the plot's events Table for text and plot relevance Stated versus implied, personal connections instead of text dependency Under the Lemon Moon (Fine, 1999; entry text) Enemy Pie (Munson, 2000; shared and modeled) The Watsons Go to Birmingham—1963 (Curtis, 2013; grade-level text)
I can compare and contrast characters, ideas, and events within stories.	➡	Instructional strategies? Misconceptions? Appropriate text?	Venn diagram or T-chart, sorting by characteristics Looking at traits only, or confusing characters when pronouns are present Enemy Pie (Munson, 2000; shared and modeled) The Watsons Go to Birmingham—1963 (Curtis, 2013; grade-level text)
I can infer meaning in text and cite evidence to support my thinking.	➡	Instructional strategies? Misconceptions? Appropriate text?	Connections to plot, plot mapping; annotate! Not being text dependent or thinking around theme or plot, listing details that don't align The Watsons Go to Birmingham—1963 (Curtis, 2013; grade-level text)

Source for standard: NGA & CCSSO, 2010.

After literacy teams have studied, analyzed, deconstructed, and reconstructed the essential literacy standards, they are equipped to transfer their hard work into a doable plan for teaching and learning. Literacy teachers who engage in the collaborative process of creating a guaranteed and viable curriculum gain clarity and expertise in designing literacy learning that takes the guesswork out of ensuring all students are learning at high levels.

Get Going or Get Better

As you think about your systems and structures to support literacy teams in ensuring that all students are reading at high levels, what changes, refinements, or complete overhauls would help teams ensure a guaranteed and viable curriculum on your campus? Use the reproducible "Get Going on Chapter 2: Ensure a Guaranteed and Viable Curriculum" as a reflection tool for the learning in chapter 2 to move forward in the collaborative work of literacy teams.

Get Going on Chapter 2:
Ensure a Guaranteed and Viable Curriculum

> » Is instructional reading time in your master schedule protected and sufficient in order to make the curriculum viable? Several research studies suggest ninety uninterrupted minutes (Underwood, 2018).
>
> » Does your guaranteed and viable curriculum include each of the five critical components of (1) phonemic awareness, (2) phonics, (3) fluency, (4) vocabulary, and (5) comprehension (National Reading Panel, 2000)? Does the proportion of instructional time allocated to each component shift as students move from beginning readers to proficient readers and incorporate oral language development throughout?
>
> » How has your team engaged in the work of sorting standards into those that are guaranteed, engaged, and introduced? Is everyone on the team clear on what is essential?
>
> » Has the team mapped out the essential standards across the year so everyone knows when to expect student proficiency for the essential standard learning targets?
>
> » Does the team use collaborative time to engage in rich conversations that build shared expertise on the essentials by deconstructing them into learning targets and learning progressions?

Getting Started?	Getting Better?
Sometimes it is best to go slow to go fast (Senge, 1990). While it may be hard for teachers to put standards into the "important" category when they seem so essential, it's better for teams to be able to grow through this process on a smaller number of essential standards this year than to take on too many essentials. We recommend choosing one essential standard per genre or unit that will be the focus of collaborative time; then next year revisit the list of essentials and add more as the teams are ready.	We have found that this process is ongoing and recursive. Each year, teams should revisit and refine their essential standards lists to align with what the teams are ready to study during their collaborative time and guarantee in their instruction. Consider digging deeper into the embedded and recursive standards and looking across the year at how essential standards can be more intentionally incorporated into each unit and into other content areas. (Think informational text skills in science and social studies.)

References

National Reading Panel. (2000). *Teaching children to read: An evidence-based assessment of the scientific research literature on reading and its implications for reading instruction—Reports of the subgroups.* Bethesda, MD: National Institute of Child Health and Human Development. Accessed at www.nichd.nih.gov/sites /default /files/publications/pubs/nrp/Documents/report.pdf on October 10, 2022.

Senge, P. M. (1990). *The fifth discipline: The art and practice of the learning organization.* New York: Doubleday.

Underwood, S. (2018, January). *What is the evidence for an uninterrupted, 90-minute literacy instruction block?* [Brief]. Portland, OR: Education Northwest. Accessed at https://educationnorthwest.org/sites/default /files/resources/uninterrupted-literacy-block-brief.pdf on January 11, 2023.

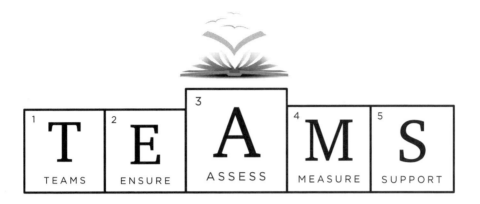

TEAMS | ENSURE | ASSESS | MEASURE | SUPPORT

CHAPTER 3

Assess and Monitor Student Reading Achievement With Ongoing Assessment

We are curious. Are you heading into this chapter on the topic of assessment with anticipation or dread? You see, assessment gets a lot of bad press among educators. Many educators question why their districts require so much testing that it takes time away from teaching. They bristle at using end-of-year standardized assessments to judge the success of an entire year's worth of learning when that paints such an incomplete picture of students and their growth. Others are data geeks who are hungry for assessment information that helps them adjust their lessons for better results. When adults think about assessment, some still carry the angst of getting back their own papers marked in red pointing out everything they got wrong.

We understand that the topic of reading assessments elicits a variety of responses and may come with some baggage. It is crucial that we adults unpack that baggage and rethink our relationships with assessment for two reasons. First, assessment expert Rick Stiggins (2001) says, "You can enhance or destroy students' desire to succeed in school more quickly and permanently through your use of assessment than with any other tools you have at your disposal" (p. 36). Think about the weight of that because all the effort you invest in building relationships, engaging your students, and differentiating lessons to help them develop a love of reading and learning will be for naught if your use of assessment has a harmful impact. Reading assessments are the tools that hold the ultimate power to enhance or destroy learning.

The good news is that in a PLC at Work, getting it right is not left up to any one of us to do alone, which brings us to the second reason we need to really unpack the baggage around assessment. Richard DuFour (2016a) called common formative assessments the *linchpin* of the PLC process. Not only does assessment most greatly impact student learning, but it can have the greatest impact on the adults' professional learning when we collaborate around the data from assessments to improve individual and collective practices. Figure 3.1 shows how teacher teams use the same reading assessment (common) to improve learning (formative) by analyzing the data (assessment), which is the embodiment of the three big ideas of a PLC at Work.

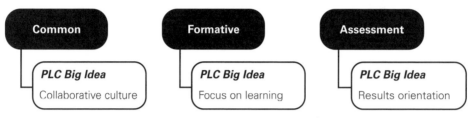

Source: *Adapted from DuFour et al., 2016; Kerr, Hulen, Heller, & Butler, 2021.*

FIGURE 3.1: Common formative assessments embody the three big ideas of a PLC at Work.

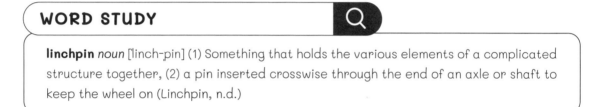

WORD STUDY

linchpin *noun* [linch-pin] (1) Something that holds the various elements of a complicated structure together, (2) a pin inserted crosswise through the end of an axle or shaft to keep the wheel on (Linchpin, n.d.)

In this chapter, we address critical question two as we discuss district, state or province, and publisher assessments and look at mindset shifts around reading assessments, as well as assessment techniques for reading and assessments *for* learning (as opposed to assessments *of* learning; Stiggins, 2005). We provide our step-by-step protocol to building common formative assessments; offer suggestions on removing barriers to valid assessment data gathering; share our step-by-step protocol to analyzing data for evidence of instructional effectiveness; and clarify how to analyze and use data from assessments to set goals with students and achieve reading goals. This chapter also includes the reproducible "Get Going on Chapter 3: Assess and Monitor Student Reading Achievement With Ongoing Assessment" (page 93).

District, State or Province, and Publisher Assessments

Common formative assessments may be the linchpin of the PLC at Work process, but they are not the only assessments used in reading. Individual teachers do quick checks for understanding during or after their lessons, but these are not necessarily *common* across classrooms in the same grade level. Teachers also administer screeners and standardized assessments required by the school, district, state, or province. These assessments are common, but they are not common formative assessments if teachers do not use them *formatively* (analyzing the data to inform instruction and impact both student and teacher learning).

While it is important for both individual teachers and school systems to collect and use reading data, the PLC at Work process emphasizes the use of team-developed assessments aligned with instruction, which allow teams to regularly assess and monitor learning, as clarified in figure 3.2.

Common	Formative	Assessment
✓		District or state or provincial standardized assessments and screeners
	✓	Individual classroom quick checks for understanding during or following a lesson or lessons
✓	✓	Team-developed or agreed-on common formative assessments on essential standards

FIGURE 3.2: Assessments may or may not be used commonly and formatively.

Why should teams build common formative assessments when there are already standardized reading assessments and publisher-created assessments? Knowledge is power, and we want the best knowledge about the effectiveness of our instruction; that enables us to create more powerful lessons designed specifically to meet students where they are according to the data and move them up the learning progression to become more proficient readers.

Mindset Shifts Around Reading Assessments

Literacy teachers are no strangers to assessment. There are norm-referenced universal reading screeners often given at the beginning of the year, reading inventories, running records, word lists, midyear progress-monitoring measures, assessments for word study and vocabulary, district benchmark comprehension assessments, and culminating end-of-year high-stakes assessments. Just as there are more reading standards than teachers can teach in a single academic year, there are more reading assessments than they can use. The kind of data that matter most center on the literacy outcomes that matter most.

While there is so much to value and learn from large-scale assessments, they do not guide teachers in the process of providing ongoing, timely feedback for essential learning outcomes in reading. Larry Ainsworth and Donald Viegut (2006) state, "Large-scale external assessments *of* learning are insufficient if the results are intended to inform current instruction and help all students improve" (p. 26).

Data from our common formative assessments are designed to inform our ability to create meaningful feedback that we share with students as partners in their reading success. These data are a critical component to the learning process and are arguably the most important source of information that supports learning (Brookhart, 2019). The only way to get data that fully align with our language of instruction is to make sure that the teachers

> The only way to get data that fully align with our language of instruction is to make sure that the teachers who are creating that instruction are also creating the assessment.

who are creating that instruction are also creating the assessment. As Paul Black and Dylan Wiliam (2010) state, "What emerges very clearly here is the indivisibility of instruction and formative assessment practices." Table 3.1 shows the shifts in mindset as teams embrace this idea and grow in their use of common formative assessments.

TABLE 3.1: Ten Shifts in the Cultural Mindsets Around Reading Assessment

From This . . .	. . . To This
Overreliance on infrequent large-scale screeners or comprehension summative assessments	Utilization of frequent common formative assessments aligned with essential reading standards, target by target
Reading assessments to determine which students failed by the end of the week, unit, or marking period	Assessments used to inform, motivate, build student efficacy, and coach students to success in essential reading standards
Reading assessments used for grades and reporting	Reading assessments used to provide meaningful and timely feedback
Reading assessments used to select students and sort them into categories of assumed potential	Reading assessments used to identify strengths and opportunities for growth
Assessing many reading skills, competencies, and dispositions at the end of a unit	Assessing a few essential reading learning targets frequently
Individual reading teachers determining success criteria for assignments and assessing work alone	Literacy teams collaboratively clarifying and determining the success criteria to ensure consistency when assessing the work
Overreliance on one kind of reading assessment	Balanced reliance on multiple types of assessments appropriate to learning standards
Focusing on averaging reading scores	Monitoring each student's reading progress toward grade-level proficiency in every essential learning target
Reading assessments determining the value of a student	Reading assessments determining best next steps for student learning
Assessing what was *taught*	Understanding what was *learned*

Source: Adapted from DuFour et al., 2016.

As you reviewed the table, did you see some cultural mindset shifts that your team has already tackled and some that your team is in the midst of addressing when you think about how you assess? Shifting cultural mindsets is an ongoing process even for teams who are far along in their PLC journey, so the tools and understandings in this chapter are designed to help your team make the next shift in your assessment practices.

Assessment Techniques for Reading

As teams move from relying on infrequent large-scale reading assessments to more frequent team-developed common formative assessments, there are several techniques for collecting the data they seek. Consider when it is appropriate to use performance-based assessment and student independent response.

Performance-Based Assessment

By observing students perform a specific task such as sorting letters or words, blending sounds in sequence, reading aloud, or retelling a story, teachers can record data about student learning. This is an especially important assessment technique with younger learners for whom independent response is not yet developmentally appropriate. Teacher observations and reading conferences are performance-based assessments.

TEACHER OBSERVATION

After explaining a task, the teacher gives no more prompts or supports. That way, the teacher can observe what the student does independently and record performance data on a common recording sheet such as a checklist, running record, or continuum. Once the team commonly develops the recording form, each individual teacher can use it not just as a one-time assessment but continue adding data during observations over a day or two.

READING CONFERENCE

Teams generate questions or prompts for students to respond to orally and record responses as data. The conference can sound like an interview with a back-and-forth volley of questions and answers. Or it can be set up to flow more like a conversation where the assessor may stop after just a question or two if they have gotten the necessary information, or the assessor may ask clarifying questions or provide prompts to further probe the student's level of understanding. This is an important assessment technique because it has been our experience that writing is not a preferred task for many students. Assessing reading comprehension by asking students to write about what they read does not always show what they truly understand if the act of writing gets in the way of a fully developed response.

Student Independent Response

While this used to be referred to as a *pencil-and-paper task*, many independent response assessments are done on an electronic device. Because of that, teachers must carefully consider not only the questions they are asking but also the tools that some or all students may need available during the assessment. These accommodations are provided as supports to ensure students have access to the grade-level text and task. Accommodations remove learning barriers in the classroom to provide every student with equal access to learning (Reading Rockets, n.d.a). These accommodations do not alter *what* the students must learn, but provide necessary adjustments in *how* they will demonstrate the learning (The Understood Team, n.d.).

Some common reading assessment accommodations include access to the text (scrolling back, a split screen, text to talk, large print), tracking cards to slide under the text, the ability to highlight or underline text, and the amount of space available to record their response.

SELECTED RESPONSE

Multiple-choice, true/false, and sometimes fill-in-the-blank questions (if a word bank or other support is provided) are frequently used when teams want to standardize an independent response assessment across classes. This is because teachers can more easily calibrate scoring when the answer choices are provided than when students construct their own answers.

CONSTRUCTED RESPONSE

Just as students orally construct their response in a reading conference, this type of assessment asks them to think about constructing an original response, but in written form. Depending on the purpose of the assessment, the response could vary from just a word that completes a sentence to a multi-paragraph summary and analysis of text.

Think back to the critical components of reading (phonemic awareness, phonics, fluency, vocabulary, and comprehension) plus the foundation of oral language development, and consider which techniques you currently use to assess essential standards in each category. Elementary teachers generally rely more heavily on performance-based assessment since students have not yet developed the writing skills to fully show what they know, while upper-grade teachers appreciate the time-saving factor of assessing all students at once when they each record their own independent responses.

Use figure 3.3 to broaden your team's repertoire of assessment techniques by asking how you could gather data for your current essential standards in multiple ways across all the components of reading.

	Oral Language	Phonemic Awareness	Phonics	Fluency	Vocabulary	Comprehension
Performance-Based Assessment	Observe or confer?	Observe or confer?	Observe or confer?	Observe or confer?	Observe or confer?	Observe or confer?
Student Independent Response	Select or construct response?	Select or construct response?	Select or construct response?	Select or construct response?	Select or construct response?	Select or construct response?

FIGURE 3.3: Assessment options for consideration form.

*Visit **go.SolutionTree.com/literacy** for a free reproducible version of this figure.*

Whichever assessment technique your team chooses, the act of learning and the act of assessing should not be separate. Students do not have to stop their learning for teachers to take time out of instruction to perform assessments. If students are actively engaged in a learning task, then teachers can observe their actions without interfering (observation assessment technique) or ask about their learning (interview or conference assessment technique) while the rest of the class continues with the task (which may be an independent response).

Assessment Planning by Learning Target

When answering critical question two of the PLC at Work process, teams take all the shared knowledge built by answering question one and create a collaborative plan for measuring, responding to, and developing learning. In this way, teachers are students of assessment, so they can ensure they are bringing high-quality assessments to their students.

Adding the assessment component of their teaching and learning plan requires teams to engage in that additional layer of depth and clarity around each literacy learning target. As in chapter 2 (page 35), we ask teams to apply the four critical questions of learning in the PLC at Work process for each step of student learning. In building common formative assessments aligned with specific learning targets, teams front-load conversations about possible classroom quick checks for understanding as well as common formative assessment ideas before teaching the lessons. They determine if learning targets need to be assessed on the common assessment, and if so, how. If teams are able to clarify assessment needs at each step in the learning progression, then they can swiftly and adeptly respond to that information as students engage in the learning.

Teachers use *classroom quick checks* in the following ways.

- Teacher-created informal, frequent measures of learning

- Tool to discover where classroom students are in the learning as they are learning it

- Opportunities to seek out multiple data points in multiple ways

- Information on how to respond to individual students' needs and strengths

- Planning tool for the next level of instruction, support, and response to learning

Teams use *common formative assessments* in the following ways.

- Team-created formal measure of essential learning

- Tool to discover where all grade-level or content-area students are in the learning as determined by paced markers in the learning cycle

- Opportunities to review data points that align with specific measures of learning in team agreed-on ways

- Information on how to respond to individual students' needs and strengths

- Planning tool to inform team responses to instructional needs, additional supports, and collective responses to learning

- Learning tool to provide insights on strengths and opportunities regarding each teacher's professional practices in ensuring mastery of essential reading standards

It is important to note that the collaborative work of determining how you will know when students have or have not learned must be done *prior* to beginning the unit. Designing and developing assessments while you are in the current teaching and learning cycle is like trying to fix a flat tire while the car is moving. Teams always aim to be ahead of the learning in order to be better prepared to respond to the learning.

The example in figure 3.4 (page 70) illustrates how teams would approach this work target by target, addressing essential conversations of critical question two. See appendix B for the reproducible "Building an Assessment Plan by Learning Target: Critical Question Two (Show)" (page 147).

Unit: Nonfiction unit one

Essential Literacy Standard: RI.3.2—Determine the main idea of a text; recount the key details and explain how they support the main idea.

Learning Target		Question Two: Show	Team Notes
I can determine the topic and purpose.	→	How will we assess on common formative assessments? Ideas for quick checks? Appropriate text?	Common formative assessment task: Determine topic and purpose, create main idea statement, select main idea. Quick check: Graphic organizer or T-chart (Find main idea in short text in isolation and move into larger chunks of text. Multiple choice is an option for students who need a place to start.) Instructional texts: multiple short grade-level texts
I can identify key details that support the main idea.	→	How will we assess on common formative assessments? Ideas for quick checks? Appropriate text?	Common formative assessment task: Use familiar texts that have established main ideas. Quick checks: Lists, table organizer, and annotations Instructional texts: "Star Parties," pp. 9–13 (Texas Education Agency, 2018) "Lost and Found," pp. 9–14 (Texas Education Agency, 2017)
I can explain why each detail supports the topic and purpose.	→	How will we assess on common formative assessments? Ideas for quick checks? Appropriate text?	Common formative assessment task: Use open response for detail and multiple choice for how it supports. Quick checks: Annotations and thinking map Instructional texts: "Star Parties," pp. 9–13 (Texas Education Agency, 2018) "Lost and Found," pp. 9–14 (Texas Education Agency, 2017)
I can cite textual evidence to support my thinking.	→	How will we assess on common formative assessments? Ideas for quick checks? Appropriate text?	Common formative assessment task: Cite text for each answer with open-ended response; two or three selected responses with distractors. Quick checks: "Oh Yeah? Prove It!" chart and annotations Instructional texts: "Star Parties," pp. 9–13 (Texas Education Agency, 2018) "Lost and Found," pp. 9–14 (Texas Education Agency, 2017)

Source for standard: NGA & CCSSO, 2010.

FIGURE 3.4: Third-grade team example of building an assessment plan by learning target—Critical question two (show).

TEAMS Process Protocol for Building Common Formative Assessments

Engaging in effective collaboration around creating a complete assessment plan for an essential literacy standard is a complex process that takes practice and patience, so we've developed a step-by-step protocol specific to literacy outcomes to help guide teams. As mentioned earlier, compliance is not the goal, so this is not intended to be a "fill in the blanks and turn it in" document. This tool is meant to be used as a discussion guide for teams to gain clarity and expertise on meaningful assessment outcomes. Depending on the teams' skills, this tool may be heavily utilized to help start teams in the right direction or lightly reviewed to ensure well-versed teams are hitting the mark in their collective work. Think about where your team is in the process as you read the steps in the protocol.

A brief summary of the steps follows.

- **Steps 1–3** ask teams to label the focus of the assessment template and list the essential literacy standard that will be assessed. Teams will agree on locked-in dates for the collective administration of common formative assessments. This allows teams to organize their assessment timeline to map out the instructional cycle for each learning target and to include opportunities for *classroom* formative assessments and responsive feedback before each *common* formative assessment.

- **Steps 4–6** ask teams to apply their work from collaboratively deconstructing the standard and studying assessment examples to create or curate an assessment and connect it to the rigor and expectations of end-of-unit, summative, or large-scale assessments. What language of assessment and academic vocabulary should we mirror? How complex is the text? What can teams learn about how students will engage in the tasks? What is the expectation of rigor? Teams will also align each learning target with an appropriate method of assessment that will provide the most information for responding to student learning.

- **Steps 7–8** ask teams to review and refine their assessment through the lens of learners. Teams take the assessment and check for clarity, cohesion, and alignment. Teams ensure each question or task meets the criteria for proficiency. What would be the best answer and why? What would be the best *worst* answer and why? From the teams' collective review, changes and refinements are made to ensure that the test is valid.

- **Steps 9–10** ask teams to collectively determine and agree on success criteria for each level of student proficiency and calibrate how they will measure and record learning. Teams must collectively agree on what proficiency is before they can equitably guarantee it. Additionally, teams agree on consistent administration guidelines to ensure results are truly comparable.

Here is the protocol for building common formative assessments, which also appears as the reproducible "TEAMS Process Protocol for Building Common Formative Assessments" (page 139) in appendix A.

1. **Name** the unit by genre or focus, and list the essential standards that will be assessed and the date of the summative unit assessment. Determine the tentative dates for common formative assessments within the unit.

2. **Pace** the teaching, assessing, and response to each learning target within the essential literacy standard by deciding how many days of instruction will be dedicated to each of the learning targets and which learning targets will be included on the common formative assessments.

3. **Align** with available assessment blueprints or released assessment items for expectations of rigor, text complexity, and academic vocabulary and models of assessment questions.

4. **Format** the assessment, choosing the most appropriate method or design in order to have the best opportunity to gain insight on student learning and provide feedback.

5. **Select** appropriate texts to be used if assessing for comprehension, specifically evaluating the text complexity and purpose to be sure students can access the text and show what they comprehend.

6. **Create** or curate the common formative assessment, building the questions, answer stems, tasks, or prompts, or collectively determining which premade or prepublished assessment meets the agreed-on criteria and if it needs to be adapted in any way.

7. **Review** the assessment by having all teachers on the team take the test as if they were students to identify any possible edits or revisions. Have teachers determine the *best* answer choice as a key and the best *incorrect* answer to explain why students would make the error.

8. **Refine** and revise as necessary. Assign individual team members action steps and a timeline for completion if necessary before publishing the assessment.

9. **Determine** how to score the assessment by creating a checklist, proficiency scale, or rubric with clearly articulated success criteria.

10. **Calibrate** the scoring guide, and proactively determine how to assign points, give credit, or make determinations of proficiency. How will the team manage accommodations for students with IEP or 504 eligibility? Will other literacy skills such as grammar and punctuation be measured on this assessment?

Figure 3.5 provides an example of a completed template so you can see how a team's discussion might be documented. The responses may not be what your team would have collectively determined, but the process of *how* this team worked through the shared learning is the most important takeaway. See appendix B for the customizable reproducible "TEAMS Process Template: Building Common Formative Assessments" (page 148).

1. **Name** unit assessment: Nonfiction informative or expository text Essential literacy standard assessed: RI.3.2: main idea, key details		Embedded and recursive essential literacy standards assessed: RI.3.1: Ask, answer, and cite RI.3.4: Determine word meaning in context		
Date of common formative assessments: November 18 Date of team data reviews: November 23		Date of summative or unit assessment: December 3 (all nonfiction essentials)		
2. **Pace** teaching, learning, assessing, and response (essential standard pacing map):				
Day 1 I can determine topic and purpose.	Day 2 I can determine topic and purpose.	Day 3 Quick Check: I can determine topic and purpose.	Day 4 Quick Check Response: I can determine topic and purpose.	Day 5 I can identify key details in text. I can determine word meaning in context.
Day 6 I can identify key details in text. I can determine word meaning in context.	Day 7 I can identify key details in text.	Day 8 Quick Check: I can identify key details in text. I can determine word meaning in context.	Day 9 Quick Check Response: I can identify key details in text. New learning: I can explain how key details support the topic and purpose.	Day 10 I can explain how key details support the topic and purpose. I can support my thinking with text evidence.

FIGURE 3.5: Building common formative assessments protocol—Third-grade example.

continued ▶

Day 11	Day 12	Day 13	Day 14	Day 15
I can explain how key details support the topic and purpose. I can support my thinking with text evidence.	Quick Check: I can explain how key details support the topic and purpose. I can support my thinking with text evidence.	Quick Check Response: I can explain how key details support the topic and purpose. I can support my thinking with text evidence.	Putting It All Together: Review and refine with new nonfiction text.	Common Formative Assessment: I can determine topic and purpose. I can identify key details in text. I can determine word meaning in context. I can explain how key details support the topic and purpose. I can support my thinking with text evidence.

3. **Align** with assessment blueprints by finding examples of the following (check all that apply):

☑ Rigor ☐ Tasks or behaviors ☐ Text complexity ☑ Academic vocabulary

Notes:

Grade-level text is stated, main idea implied in end-of-year level texts. Some questions include tricky details. It asks for main idea of sections and paragraphs, main idea of whole text or passage not found.

Must identify topic and purpose, then create or choose main idea statement.

Academic vocabulary added.

4. **Format** assessment design:

Learning target one:

I can determine the topic and purpose.

Check all that apply:

☐ Performance ☐ Selected response ☑ Constructed response

Notes:

Graphic organizer

Write main idea statement

Learning target two:

I can identify key details.

Check all that apply:

☐ Performance ✓ Selected response ✓ Constructed response

Notes:

Graphic organizer, annotations, list of key details, multiple choice

- -

Learning target three:

I can explain how key details support the topic and purpose and I can support my thinking with text evidence.

Check all that apply:

☐ Performance ☐ Selected response ✓ Constructed response

Notes:

Graphic organizer, annotations, list of key details, open-ended response, multiple choice

5. **Select** text for this assessment:

Wild Weather: Hurricanes! by Lorraine Jean Hopping (1995) *(on target)*

Ultimate Jungle Rumble: Who Would Win? by Jerry Pallotta (2018) *(stretch)*

6. **Create** assessment, ensuring it matches grade-level expectations of the following (check all that apply):

✓ Rigor

✓ Tasks or behaviors

✓ Complexity of text

✓ Academic vocabulary

Link for created or curated assessment: Click here

7. **Review** notes from team observations:

Students have a lot of content vocabulary to wade through; beef up connection of key details and determining word meaning in context.

Open ended may be less complex for students because key details sound like the topic and purpose in multiple choice.

Best worst answers were all details and did not indicate author's purpose. (Note heavily in instruction!)

Students will be able to cite text evidence, but must go back to correct section subheading.

continued ▶

8. **Refine** and revise as needed:	Team member assigned:
Change Habitat subheading and insert new heading into the question stem for 5. Correct capitalization error 3. Remove multiple choice 7 to make open ended.	Christine

9. **Determine** success criteria:

Level 3 descriptors for attaining grade-level proficiency:

Determines topic and purpose and crafts main idea statement

Key details consistently align with the topic and purpose, and explanation of how the detail supports the main idea is provided.

Text evidence is aligned and focused.

Level 2 descriptors for progressing grade-level proficiency:

Recognizes topic and determines purpose and crafts simple main idea statement

Key details are identified and mostly align with the topic and purpose.

Some explanation is provided on how the key detail supports the topic and purpose, but may include extra details or details that do not match.

Text evidence is oversimplified or not provided.

Level 1 descriptors for emerging grade-level proficiency:

Recognizes topic but has difficulty determining purpose

Some key details are identified, but does not yet explain how the detail supports the main idea.

Finding evidence to support text is a challenge.

10. **Calibrate** scoring agreements:

Word meaning assessed on RI.3.4 proficiency scale, score all sections completed. If a student did not finish, score what was completed and note "extra time needed" on student's reading task/behavior goals.

Test administration agreements:

No support provided for unknown words in order to gather data for determining word meaning in context. One class period provided for completion unless noted by IEP/504, privacy offices up. Considerations for accommodations:

IEP/504 eligibility: Read entire passage once and students annotate text independently (no support with annotations). Students reread independently. Read questions and answers for identified students (student paced).

Source for standards: NGA & CCSSO, 2010.

What about assessments that measure a bigger scope of learning? If teams are developing a common unit, genre study, or summative assessment, the same template and team discussion guide would apply. While we have not included a broad-view example of a team's completed end-of-unit or end-of-genre assessment plan, the collaborative process remains the same.

How to Remove Barriers to Gathering Valid Assessment Data

After your team has gone through the steps collaboratively and worked so hard to create a quality assessment, you want to ensure you've got valid and reliable data to inform your instruction. Having validity means the assessment actually measures what you want it to, and reliability ensures the assessment yields accurate data (Marzano, 2018). However, there is one more thing to consider before administering the assessment: your students. When determining the best assessment techniques, tasks, and tools to use, consider what barriers may get in the way of getting valid data about what a student truly knows and is able to do in reading. For example, when working with first graders, consider if they have the writing skills necessary to communicate their comprehension on paper or if they have the technology skills and self-regulation necessary to take an assessment on a computer. When working with teachers of older students, the trickiest aspect of assessment we get asked about (over and over in school after school) goes something like this: "If students are currently reading more than a year below grade level and we want to assess reading comprehension skills such as summarizing, determining main idea, and identifying theme, how do we collect data for those students who cannot decode grade-level text on a common formative assessment in order to correctly answer the comprehension questions about the passage?"

First of all, bravo to those teams struggling with this question. You understand the very important premise that students who read below grade level do not think below grade level. It is misplaced sympathy to lower comprehension expectations for students who have decoding difficulties since all students, regardless of current reading level, should be expected to become proficient at the essential grade-level comprehension standards. And many students can show proficiency for comprehension standards even while they are still working to build up their grade-level decoding skills (Heller, 2020). In fact, when you cross decoding skills

> Students who read below grade level do not think below grade level. It is misplaced sympathy to lower comprehension expectations for students who have decoding difficulties.

with comprehension skills, you end up with the four quadrants of reading profiles shown in figure 3.6 (page 78). You can probably think of students you've taught who fit into each of the four quadrants.

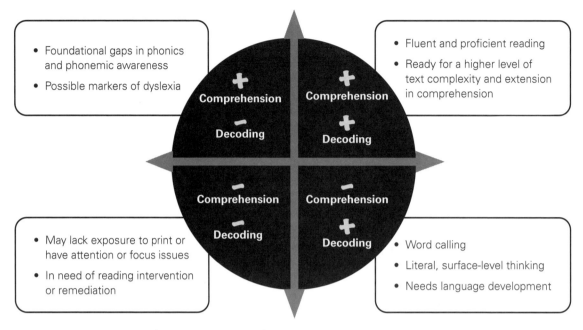

- Foundational gaps in phonics and phonemic awareness
- Possible markers of dyslexia

+ Comprehension
– Decoding

+ Comprehension
+ Decoding

- Fluent and proficient reading
- Ready for a higher level of text complexity and extension in comprehension

– Comprehension
– Decoding

– Comprehension
+ Decoding

- May lack exposure to print or have attention or focus issues
- In need of reading intervention or remediation

- Word calling
- Literal, surface-level thinking
- Needs language development

Source: Adapted from Ebert & Scott, 2016; Gough & Tunmer, 1986.

FIGURE 3.6: Quadrants of reading skills to consider when creating assessments.

The reasons a student may not yet be reading on grade level—holes in foundational skills, characteristics of dyslexia, language development, or other needs—do not necessarily prevent the student from understanding key ideas and details, analyzing an author's craft, and integrating knowledge and ideas. So you need good data, and you need to find out where the student's abilities in those areas lie while the student concurrently works to improve the skills they lack. How does your team do that?

In our experience, the following are the five most common approaches that teams take when trying to remove barriers for students who have trouble accessing the grade-level text on a comprehension common formative assessment (Heller, 2020).

1. Read the passage aloud to everyone if there are many students in the class who are currently decoding below grade level.

2. Read the passage aloud or have an audio recording for students who cannot decode text while the rest of the class reads the passage independently.

3. Provide accommodations to students who cannot decode. The accommodations should give those students the ability to access the text independently, such as previewing it with the teacher and discussing words that may be challenging, or attempting to read it before the assessment and asking the teacher for help on words or phrases they cannot decode.

4. Develop a second version of the assessment for students who cannot access the grade-level passage that asks questions on the same skill but uses an easier-to-read passage.

> **5.** Give the students reading below grade level the same assessment without accommodations, and see what they can do; by the end of the year, they are expected to independently show comprehension of grade-level text.

What does your team usually do? Is it working for you? Is it working for your students? How do you know? Each of these approaches has its shortcomings, as seen in table 3.2.

TABLE 3.2: Pros and Cons of Approaches to Assessing the Comprehension of Students Decoding Below Grade Level

Approach	Pros	Cons
Grade-level passage read aloud to all	All students take the same assessment with the same level of rigor of questions for the comprehension standard.	It assesses listening comprehension as opposed to reading comprehension. It does not match the rigor of what the students authentically do when they independently read and comprehend.
Grade-level passage read aloud to some	It aligns with what the majority of students do (read and comprehend) while giving valid comprehension data for those with decoding difficulties.	It builds dependency on the teacher to read for them. It is difficult to manage when some students are reading to themselves and some are being read to.
Accommodations given to students so they can access the text	It provides students with what they need to independently complete the assessment to the best of their ability.	It is time consuming to provide preview time before the assessment. It is difficult to keep consistent across the team since some teachers may provide more support than others unless criteria are clearly determined.
Easier passage read independently	It provides an opportunity for students to show what they read and comprehend independently.	It results in less reliable data, since easier passages often are more explicit, thus lowering the rigor of the comprehension skills. It is extra work to create two quality versions of reading assessments. It is difficult to find passages at various reading levels in the same genre with the same familiarity of student background knowledge.
No accommodation made	It matches what students will have to do on end-of-year summative assessments.	Invalid data may inappropriately put students who need decoding intervention into needless comprehension intervention groups. The social-emotional impact may increase reading frustration and lower students' self-images as readers if they cannot access the text in order to show what they can comprehend.

Source: Adapted from Heller, 2020.

The approach you take for any given assessment cannot be a decision that individual teachers make. If they do make it, the formative assessment data will not be *common*. Teams make this decision together. With increasing access to technology in the classroom, there are a plethora of options that allow students to pause and replay sections of text as well as online resources for leveled passages, so you must get in the habit of considering new ways to get the best data possible for your students and your team.

TEAMS Process Protocol for Analyzing Data for Evidence of Instructional Effectiveness (Steps 1–5)

Our colleague Katie White (personal communication, 2019), who is a passionate thought leader in assessment, refers to analyzing student data as *harvesting strengths*. Shifting mindsets on traditional assessments requires teams to embrace assessment as an opportunity to *improve* learning while noting the strengths (reading skills and proficiencies) students have already developed. While the next chapter focuses on how teams collectively respond to common formative assessment data, we want to provide a tool that helps teachers develop a plan of action for each student as they collect information on where individual students are in the learning progression for an essential reading standard by name, strength, and need.

This chapter focuses on assessment through the lens of teams collectively analyzing data to improve learning for all students in essential reading outcomes. The next chapter moves teams beyond student needs and focuses on the process of studying data to improve professional practices. While we believe the processes are interconnected, we have separated the work into two parts so teams can develop collaborative skills in a layered approach. The protocol helps guide team discussions and decisions when responding as students do and do not learn. This work creates an actionable plan and collective response to ensure learning.

As with previous protocols, a summary of the steps follows.

- **Step 1** asks teams to label the focus of the reading assessment data. What evidence was gathered and analyzed?

- **Steps 2–3** ask teams to review data and evidence of learning to determine celebrations of overall student reading achievement and growth as well as the most prevalent opportunities for improvement. Where were the most gains? Were common misconceptions proactively addressed? Where are our greatest opportunities for growth?

- **Steps 4–5** ask teams to organize needed reading support by student, standard, learning target, and need. Teams apply their collaborative work on critical question one to determine which acceleration strategies toward proficiency and extension beyond proficiency will be most effective. How will all students move forward? What strategies will be most effective?

Here are the first five steps of the protocol for analyzing data for evidence of instructional effectiveness to improve student outcomes. These steps also appear in the reproducible "TEAMS Process Protocol for Analyzing Data for Evidence of Instructional Effectiveness" (page 140) in appendix A. Steps 6–10 appear in chapter 4 (page 104), which focuses on improving teaching outcomes.

1. **Name** the unit by genre or focus, and list the essential standards and learning targets that were assessed.

2. **Celebrate** reading data to determine overall gains and strengths as a grade level and for each class. All classes and students are accounted for.

3. **Discover** overall areas in need of continued support as a grade level and for each class. Ensure all classes and students are accounted for.

4. **Organize** support by student, by learning target, and by proficiency level (need).

5. **Plan** responses by determining which strategies will be most effective to respond when students do and do not learn.

Figure 3.7 is an example of a first-grade literacy team's use of this protocol. See appendix B for the customizable reproducible "TEAMS Process Template: Analyzing Data for Evidence of Instructional Effectiveness" (page 151).

1. **Name** unit assessment: Decode one-syllable words. Essential literacy standard assessed: RF.I.3.E: Decode regularly spelled one-syllable words that follow syllable types: closed syllable.	Embedded and recursive essential literacy standards assessed: RF.I.3: Know and apply grade-level phonics and word analysis skills in decoding words. RF.I.4: Read grade-level text with sufficient accuracy and fluency to support comprehension.
2. **Celebrate** overall student strengths: Identifying and saying short vowel sounds Strategies for letter-sound identification are working in small-group instruction. Segmenting and tapping out phonemes Eight students moved from level 2 to level 3 on this assessment.	
3. **Discover** overall student opportunities: Blending CVC fluently and moving beyond saying phonemes in isolation Automaticity	

FIGURE 3.7: Analyzing data for evidence of instructional effectiveness protocol— Steps 1–5 example.

continued ▶

4. **Organize** support by student and by learning target:			
Learning Target One I can identify and say the five short vowel sounds.	**Students at Level 1: Emerging** Harry Vivian	**Students at Level 2: Progressing** Preeti Michael Jorge Preston	**Students at Level 3: Attaining** Brandon Ishmael CJ Brandy Brent Maria Angel Melissa Aaron Hanh Shruthi Tracey Jenny Carli Hai Tanner Jeff Fashid Emmanuel Sophia Douglas Esme Keisha Erik Rhea Connor Don Dante Jontavia Ron Sarai
Learning Target Two I can tap out and blend the sounds in CVC words.	**Students at Level 1: Emerging** Harry Vivian Preeti Michael Jorge Preston	**Students at Level 2: Progressing** Dante Tanner Ron Fashid Aaron Carli Esme Sophia Erik CJ Connor Brandon Don	**Students at Level 3: Attaining** Brent Rhea Angel Sarai Hai Jontavia Shruthi Ishmael Jenny Hanh Jeff Brandy Emmanuel Maria Douglas Melissa Keisha Tracey
Learning Target Three I can read CVC words with short vowel sounds.	**Students at Level 1: Emerging** Harry Carli Vivian Sophia Preeti Brandon Michael CJ Jorge Don Preston Rhea Tanner Sarai Fashid	**Students at Level 2: Progressing** Dante Jeff Ron Emmanuel Aaron Douglas Esme Keisha Erik Hanh Connor Brandy Jontavia Maria Jenny Tracey	**Students at Level 3: Attaining** Brent Angel Hai Shruthi Ishmael Melissa

5. **Plan** effective actions to accelerate learning:	Effective actions to extend learning:
Cueing cards Pushing through the letters with a reading finger Buddy reading Continued support in decodable text	Scavenger hunt in non-decodable text for words that follow the CVC pattern Reader's theater Identifying the CVC pattern in compound words

Source for standards: Arkansas Department of Education, n.d.

After getting the big picture of what students did overall and developing a plan of action to respond by name and by need, teams collectively build a planned response to ensure all students reach proficiency in essential reading outcomes. Teams share ideas, resources, and effective strategies to customize responses for individual students.

In addition to the team-developed common formative assessment, teachers can use multiple data points over time to collect information on their students' learning and progress. The reproducible "Path to Proficiency Plan Template" (page 155) provides a simple template that might help. Teachers and teams may decide to have fewer checkpoints or more frequent checkpoints depending on the complexity of the essential standard and learning targets required, as well as the student's individual needs.

An example of how a teacher or team might complete the template for an individual student in grades 3–6 based on an essential reading comprehension standard appears in figure 3.8.

Student	J'Dasia K.	
Essential Standard	Determine main idea and key details, and explain how each detail supports the topic and purpose of text.	
Learning Targets Focus	I can explain how each detail supports the topic and purpose. I can cite evidence to support my thinking.	
Proficiency Level	Choose one. ☐ Level 1: Emerging ☑ Level 2: Progressing ☐ Level 3: Attaining	
Student Strengths	Strong decoding and reading fluency skills Vocabulary and word meaning in context consistently at or above grade-level proficiency	
Action Plan	Teacher actions: Provide shorter chunks of texts for practice, and guided practice in meaningful annotations; model graphic organizer for connections to text.	Student actions: Make meaningful annotations, refer back to main idea chart, use graphic organizer to make clear connections to text, practice chunking large text into smaller pieces.
Check-In Dates	Date of checkpoint one: December 3 Date of checkpoint two: December 11 Date of checkpoint three: December 16	
Proficiency at Checkpoint One	Choose one. ☐ Level 1: Emerging ☑ Level 2: Progressing ☐ Level 3: Attaining	Checkpoint one notes: Annotations are improving, still providing nonessential information as evidence. Better with short texts, working toward longer texts.

FIGURE 3.8: Path to proficiency plan—Grades 3–6 reading comprehension example.

continued ▶

| Proficiency at Checkpoint Two | Choose one.
☐ Level 1: Emerging
☐ Level 2: Progressing
☐ Level 3: Attaining | Checkpoint two notes: |
| Proficiency at Checkpoint Three | Choose one.
☐ Level 1: Emerging
☐ Level 2: Progressing
☐ Level 3: Attaining | Checkpoint three notes: |

An example of how a teacher or team might complete the template for an individual student in early literacy grades based on an essential first-grade foundational reading standard appears in figure 3.9.

Student	Pham D.
Essential Standard	RF.I.3.E: Decode regularly spelled one-syllable words that follow syllable types (closed syllable, open syllable, vowel-consonant-e, vowel teams, consonant-le, and r-controlled vowel).
Learning Targets Focus	I can identify and say the five short vowel sounds. I can tap out and blend the sounds in CVC words. I can read CVC words with short vowel sounds. I can identify and say the five long vowel sounds. I can read open syllable words with long vowel sounds.
Proficiency Level	Choose one. ☑ Level 1: Emerging Can identify short vowels and tap out sounds in words; working on blending and reading CVC words ☐ Level 2: Progressing Can blend and read CVC words; working on flexibly decoding both CVC and open syllable words ☐ Level 3: Attaining Can identify short and long vowels and read CVC and open syllable words
Student Strengths	Automaticity in individual phoneme recognition Alphabetic principle Responds well to partner practice
Action Plan	Teacher actions: Use multisensory tactics such as nonverbal cues for short vowel sounds, letter tiles and Elkonin boxes for blending.	Student actions: Use anchor words and nonverbal cues to help distinguish between auditorily similar short vowel sounds (e and i). Tap and blend sounds in CVC words on arm or fingers.

Check-In Dates	Date of checkpoint one: January 21 Date of checkpoint two: January 30 Date of checkpoint three: February 7	
Proficiency at Checkpoint One	Choose one. ☑ Level 1: Emerging ☐ Level 2: Progressing ☐ Level 3: Attaining	Checkpoint one notes: Short *a*, *o*, and *u* are solid, but still confusing *e* and *i*. Can blend CVC words with short *a*, *o*, and *u* if tapping own arm but not yet coordinated on fingers.
Proficiency at Checkpoint Two	Choose one. ☐ Level 1: Emerging ☐ Level 2: Progressing ☑ Level 3: Attaining	Checkpoint two notes: Coordinates blending words with automaticity, only relying on tapping out using arm or fingers occasionally. Open syllables came easily once he sorted out *e* and *i* confusion.
Proficiency at Checkpoint Three	Choose one. ☐ Level 1: Emerging ☐ Level 2: Progressing ☐ Level 3: Attaining	Checkpoint three notes:

Source for standard: NGA & CCSSO, 2010.

FIGURE 3.9: Path to proficiency plan—Grades K–2 literacy example.

Assessment's Role in Student Agency

We teachers aren't the only people becoming experts in learning. Our students are working to reach mastery-level learning in essential reading outcomes, so the information we gather on where they are in their learning must be shared with them in meaningful and engaging ways. When that is done correctly, a partnership in learning emerges. The following sections discuss student goal setting, sharing, and celebrating, as well as student self-assessment tools.

Student Goal Setting, Sharing, and Celebrating

Teams might be helping students set broad reading achievement goals based on large-scale assessment data, or smaller goals based on literacy skills and dispositions, essential reading standards, or specific learning targets. While literacy teams should develop goals that meet the SMART criteria, the options for *attainable* and *results oriented* do not apply, because the state or provincial standards already set the benchmark for student achievement at grade-level proficiency or higher. Essential grade-level reading standards are already designed to be attainable and results oriented in the structure of the grade-level scope and sequence, so the goal would be to meet those expectations. You might provide a more incremental approach to the larger goal, but the expectation does not change. Keep the process simple and ensure that every interaction with students as they track and monitor their own progress is positive, focused, and actionable.

Some example templates for students tracking their own data for broad reading goals (figure 3.10), essential unit outcomes (figure 3.11), and specific reading goals (figure 3.12, page 88) appear here.

Student Name: Davonte J.	End-of-Year Goal: I can decode regularly spelled one-syllable words to read fluently.				
	September 20 Open syllable	October 5 CVC words	October 19 CVC words	November 2 Digraphs	November 16 Blends and digraphs
Exceeding	X				
Attaining*			X		X
Progressing		X			
Emerging				X	

*The goal is for all students to reach at least the attaining level of proficiency.

Next Steps to Reach My Goal	
When I will start my step: September 21	Step 1: Tap out sounds on my fingers.
When I will start my step: November 3	Step 2: Play sh, th, ch bingo and build words at choice time.
When I will start my step:	Step 3:
How I will celebrate reaching my goal:	

FIGURE 3.10: Large goal progress-monitoring tracker.

*Visit **go.SolutionTree.com/literacy** for a free reproducible version of this figure.*

Learning Target Progression	Date Mastered
I can define characteristics of fiction texts.	
I can determine word meaning in fiction text.	
I can identify the setting.	
I can explain how the setting is important to the story.	
I can identify essential characters.	
I can identify the problem.	
I can identify the solution.	
I can identify the events in the rising action.	
I can identify the climax.	
I can identify the events in the falling action.	
I can describe the major events in a story.	
I can analyze characters' thoughts, actions, and motivations.	
I can explain the actions and interactions of characters.	
I can compare and contrast characters, ideas, and events within stories.	
I can determine the theme.	
I can compare and contrast themes across multiple texts.	
I can summarize fiction texts.	
I can infer meaning in text.	
I can cite evidence from text to support my thinking.	

Source for standard: NGA & CCSSO, 2010; Texas Education Agency, n.d.

FIGURE 3.11: Fiction-unit learning target mastery checklist.

*Visit **go.SolutionTree.com/literacy** for a free reproducible version of this figure.*

My name	
What I'm learning	Reading learning target or reading goal
Where I am in my learning	Choose one. Level 1: Emerging Date: Level 2: Progressing Date: Level 3: Attaining Date:
What I'm great at	
What I'm working on	
What I'm doing to get better	
What I did to accomplish my goal	

FIGURE 3.12: Learning goal student data tracker.

*Visit **go.SolutionTree.com/literacy** for a free reproducible version of this figure.*

Student Self-Assessment Tools

While large reading goals and unit goals are what you are working toward, if teams want to develop goal-directed students who take ownership of their learning, then focusing on tracking specific learning goals (as in figure 3.12) is the place to start. Sharing data with students and showing them how to actively take responsibility for their own learning in upcoming lessons and monitor their own growth moves them out of the trap of low achievement and develops the habits necessary to become lifelong learners (Black & Wiliam, 2010; Marzano, 2018).

It takes time and practice for students to acquire the metacognitive skills required to self-monitor learning. When teams share formative data with students, it helps to give students tools that cultivate those self-monitoring skills. The kindergarten team at Mason Crest Elementary grew this skill in students by creating goal cards that showed students exactly where they were in their learning and what their next target was in order to move toward their goal. Teachers simply took the learning target *I can* statements they'd developed when deconstructing the essential standard and added picture icons to help those students who were not yet reading be able to access the tool and have a visual reminder. You can see the first created goal card in figure 3.13.

I can identify and say the five short vowel sounds.	I can tap out the sounds in CVC words.	I can blend and read CVC words.	I can identify and say the five long vowel sounds.	I can read one-syllable words with short and long vowel sounds.
a e i o u		P A N	ā ē ī ō ū	NO
★	★	☆	☆	☆

Source: ©2023 Mason Crest Elementary School. Adapted with permission.

FIGURE 3.13: Example kindergarten goal card.

Printed on card stock in bookmark size, goal cards became a way for students to do the following.

- Talk about and have a record of their learning.

- Share their current data with any adult who may be supporting them.

- Perhaps most importantly, have concrete proof that they were growing as readers and could do hard things as teachers used a star-shaped hole punch to mark each box when a student achieved each learning target.

When those kindergartners got to first grade, they asked their teachers where their goal cards were, so the first-grade team began to use them, and the practice spread across the school. Each grade level adapted the goal cards to fit its needs. For example, first and second grade found that while kindergarten had more discreet, measurable learning targets (such as learning a certain number of letters, sounds, and high-frequency words), many of the reading skills in higher grade levels had to be continually practiced in increasingly complex text. So, rather than punching a star when a student mastered a goal, teachers used a box where they could put tally marks every time they saw a student demonstrating that skill or strategy. Figure 3.14 (page 90) is an example. This created a visual way to track which skills were well developed in the student and which skills the student was working on growing. Students could use these goal cards as self-assessment tools as well as reminders of what to focus on and practice during their independent reading time.

I can identify the characters, setting, problem, and solution.	I can describe the major events in a story.	I can analyze characters' thoughts, actions, and motivations.	I can use clues in the text to infer meaning.	I can cite evidence from text to support my thinking.
![house scene]	![story events]	![Jealous Kind]	![? boy]	![magnifying glass book]

Source: Adapted from Mason Crest Elementary School, Annandale, Virginia.

FIGURE 3.14: Example goal card with tally marks.

Another tool, often used with upper elementary students but easily adaptable to any age, is an assessment wrapper. Unlike the goal card, which spells out for students the steps of the learning progression, the assessment wrapper teaches students to go back and discover what they know and what they still need to learn after an assessment (Lovett, 2013). Figure 3.15 shows how students can use an assessment wrapper to wrap up the learning after an assessment. They analyze their correct and incorrect responses and then find celebrations, determine what they need to learn next, and make a plan for learning it. Research supports that when students engage in this kind of self-assessment, the results are increased motivation, engagement, and efficacy (Chappuis, 2014). Katie White (2022) puts it best: "when students analyze and reflect on their efforts in relation to specific goals and success criteria, they are doing so as a way to offer insight about the next instructional steps" (p. 46).

Student name:			
Directions: Color the box *green* if you answered the question correctly. Color it *red* if you answered the question incorrectly. Use your information to answer the reflection questions and make a learning plan.			
Learning Target	**Question Number**	**Question Number**	**Question Number**
I can read words with vowel-consonant-e long vowel syllables.	Question 1	Question 5	Question 7
I can read words with long vowel team syllables.	Question 3	Question 6	
I can divide a word into syllables and identify syllables with long vowel sounds.	Question 2	Question 4	

What are your strengths so far?

What do you still need to learn?

What is your goal?

What strategies will help you reach your goal?

FIGURE 3.15: Phonics assessment wrapper example.

While these samples of data trackers, goal cards, and assessment wrappers are not the only ways to develop goal-oriented learners who use formative assessment data to actively participate in their own learning, we hope they have sparked some ideas for how you could embrace this work with your team and your students.

Get Going or Get Better

As you think about your systems and structures to support literacy teams in ensuring that all students are reading at high levels, what changes, refinements, or complete overhauls would help teams create assessments that give specific data needed to monitor and improve reading achievement and set and achieve reading goals? Use the reproducible "Get Going on Chapter 3: Assess and Monitor Student Reading Achievement With Ongoing Assessment" as a reflection tool for the learning in chapter 3 to move forward in the collaborative work of literacy teams.

Get Going on Chapter 3:
Assess and Monitor Student Reading Achievement
With Ongoing Assessment

> » How is your team developing common formative assessments that align with instruction and give specific data on learning targets to improve reading achievement on the identified essential standards?

> » As your team shifts its thinking about assessment and you develop assessments for learning, are you using a variety of assessment techniques (observation, conference, selected response, and constructed response)? How do you arrive at team consensus for which assessment technique to use and why?

> » Rather than just collecting data, are you using a protocol to analyze student assessment data and monitor each student's progress toward reading proficiency?

> » Are you using data to create goal-directed learners who know what their reading goals are and can self-assess their progress toward meeting those goals?

Getting Started?	Getting Better?
Many teachers feel they already spend too much time assessing students and it takes precious time away from instruction. Sometimes you need to consider next *stops* rather than next *steps* (DeLong, 2011). If the assessments you are currently giving do not give you specific information about where each student is on the path to proficiency on your essential standards, then first consider omitting or revising assessments you've used in the past to make room for more purposeful data collection.	Be sure your team develops or revises common formative assessments *before* starting a unit so everyone on the team has a common understanding of the complexity level of text, task, or thinking expected at proficiency. As you refine assessments, be sure they do not just tell you which students are proficient and which are not; the assessments should give you specific data about which rung of the ladder each student is on toward proficiency. Many teams find it useful to include the *I can* statement above each question or task on an assessment so both teachers and students are clear on which learning target students are demonstrating.

Reference

DeLong, T. J. (2011, August 4). Three questions for effective feedback. *Harvard Business Review.* Accessed at https://hbr.org/2011/08/three-questions-for-effective-feedback on January 11, 2023.

TEAMS
1 TEAMS 2 ENSURE 3 ASSESS 4 MEASURE 5 SUPPORT

CHAPTER 4

Measure Effectiveness of Individual and Collective Teacher Practices

In the previous chapter, we explored assessment through the lens of teams collectively analyzing data to improve literacy outcomes for all *students*. This chapter shifts to studying data as evidence of the effectiveness of collective and individual literacy teaching practices. It is important to note that looking at data through the lens of collective efficacy and professional learning doesn't happen in isolation. Both lenses are deeply integrated into all data conversations. However, because we have found this is an area where even the most accomplished teams shy away from deep implementation, we want to guide teams through this work with a more focused approach.

In this chapter, we look at data study through collective inquiry, sharing scenarios of different teams; show how teams can purposefully celebrate data; and collaboratively analyze data for evidence of instructional effectiveness. This chapter also includes the reproducible "Get Going on Chapter 4: Measure Effectiveness of Individual and Collective Teacher Practices" (page 112). The focus of the chapter is on teams measuring evidence of the effectiveness of individual and collective teacher practices, the fourth of the five tight elements of teaching reading in a PLC.

Data Study Through Collective Inquiry

Data, the evidence of teams' effectiveness, must be relentlessly studied and purposefully celebrated through the lens of collective inquiry to build shared knowledge of effective literacy practices. That is important because, as Mike Mattos (2021) often states, "When teachers learn more, kids learn more."

WORD STUDY

collective inquiry *noun* [kə-ˈlek-tiv in-ˈkwī(-ə)r-ē] The collaborative process "by which educators build shared knowledge and learn together" to improve their craft (Jackson & Patankar, 2013)

Deeply examining data as a measure of how well the adults are doing in meeting shared goals requires vulnerability and mutual accountability. As a collaborative team in a PLC, you have already established common goals, collective commitments, and norms to guide your work. We highly recommend revisiting or refining your current norms to create a safe, supportive environment as teams engage in collective inquiry around effective team and teacher practices. Without these assurances, teams may be likely to engage in data discussions that derail healthy collaborative practices and disrupt the learning. More often than not, unhealthy data cultures avoid this component of the work altogether.

We have included dialogues from two grade-level teams working through literacy data protocols for you to observe. The scenarios are intended to demonstrate characteristics of effective and ineffective collaboration practices. These dialogues from team meetings also provide insights on the cultures the teams have cultivated as they have engaged in the work. While these case study transcripts focus on third- and fifth-grade teams, the foundations of the teams' conversations can apply to any grade level or content.

As you read the following two scenarios, it will be evident that they highlight two very different conversations that lead to very different outcomes. Consider the following questions as you read.

- Is the presence or absence of procedural norms and collective commitments evident in each scenario?

- How does each of the literacy teams approach comparing data?

- What markers are present to indicate a healthy or unhealthy data culture?

- Which literacy team is committed to engaging in collective inquiry and building shared expertise?

- Which team displays mutual accountability for shared literacy goals and professional effectiveness?

Scenario One: Third-Grade Team Data Discussion

Consider the following conversation from a third-grade team at a campus two years into implementing the PLC process. The team has just completed disaggregating the student reading data from a common formative assessment using a team protocol and determined student needs (see figure 4.1).

	Standard: RI.3.2—Determine the main idea of a text; recount the key details and explain how they support the main idea.				
	Date of data review: December 3				
	Team SMART goal: 85% at level 3 proficiency by April 22				
Teacher	**Learning Target One** I can determine the topic and purpose.	**Learning Target Two** I can identify key details that support the main idea.	**Learning Target Three** I can explain why each detail supports the topic and purpose.	**Learning Target Four** I can cite textual evidence to support my thinking.	**Overall**
DL	92%	88%	68%	85%	83.25%
SR	87%	90%	71%	83%	82.75%
CM	67%	56%	44%	57%	56%
SD	91%	94%	77%	81%	85.75%
Team	84.25%	82%	65%	76.5%	76.93%

Source for standard: NGA & CCSSO, 2010.

FIGURE 4.1: Data for team data discussion in scenario one.

The team has created shared flexible groups for students needing additional time and support in the essential standard based on individual goals around each learning target.

Cheryl: OK, now that we've built our learning target intervention groups, we need to review our team data. Let's look at our team and teacher data.

Before we get started, I just want to say that my class was so off the day we took this. I don't know what got into them, but they just didn't take this seriously. When I was teaching it, they really got it. I don't think 56 percent is where they really are.

Sheila: Well, overall, I think our scores look pretty good. This was a hard passage for them. The questions around target three were tough. Given all the academic vocabulary they had to tackle, I'm OK with these scores.

Dean: I agree! My scores would have definitely been higher if the passage weren't so difficult. It wasn't fair to my special ed and EL students. My general ed students did much better, so it's just the few who struggle that brought my data down.

Sue: My students did great! But they better do well because I have most of the gifted and talented kids and the advanced readers. They must have rushed through explaining why each detail supports the main idea.

Sheila: We're only about eight percentage points away from our SMART goal, so I think we will be able to get there through our intervention groups. But some targets are already over 85 percent, so we should be good by the time our end-of-year assessment gets here.

Cheryl: Does anyone else want to add a celebration or need?

Dean: I'll get with our special education teacher and let her know my kids need more help with nonfiction text. But I'll celebrate that even though our students aren't where they need to be, we are a great team. And our intervention groups are ready for Monday!

Sheila: My celebration is that data are looking much better overall. We just have one class that is still behind.

Sue: I just want to say that when we were looking at all of the students who made growth, that's the thing we have to remember. It shouldn't be about overall achievement. It should be about how the students grow.

Cheryl: Awesome! I've noted our celebrations on our agenda!

Now consider the scenario from a fifth-grade team data discussion.

Scenario Two: Fifth-Grade Team Data Discussion

This discussion is a snapshot from a fifth-grade team on what has been named a national Model PLC campus. Over a period of three years, the team members have refined their professional practices when looking at data to ensure that *learning for all* is at the center of their collective discussions. They've also just analyzed student data (figure 4.2) using a team protocol, determined student needs, and created shared flexible groups for additional support in the essential standards based on individual goals around each learning target.

	Standard: TEKS 5.3B—I can analyze the relationships of and conflicts among the characters.				

Date of data review: January 25					
Team fiction SMART goal: 90% at level 3 proficiency by April 22 **Team overall SMART goal:** 85% at level 3 proficiency in *all* essentials by May 19					

Teacher	Learning Target One	Learning Target Two	Learning Target Three	Learning Target Four	Overall
	I can analyze characters' thoughts, actions, and motivations.	I can analyze the relationships of and the conflicts of the characters in a story.	I can compare and contrast characters within stories.	I can infer meaning from text and quote textual evidence to support my thinking.	
MC	76%	78%	82%	85%	80.25%
AL	72%	91%	88%	81%	83%
LR	51%	86%	64%	48%	62.25%
KV	79%	94%	88%	91%	88%
Team	69.5%	87.25%	80.5%	76.25%	78.38%

Source for standard: Texas Education Agency, n.d.

FIGURE 4.2: Data for team data discussion in scenario two.

Notice how this conversation differs from the first.

Martha: We have a plan to address student needs, so let's reflect on our professional evidence. I want to remind everyone of our specific norms when we grow together professionally from data: evidence only; none of us is as great as all of us; focus on what we can control; no blame, low expectations, or competition allowed; inquiry based, solution focused, and learning centered. We use reset and thank you, resetting when we need to remind each other. Agreed?

All: Agreed.

Martha: First, I'd like us to look at our team data for TEKS 5.3B. Take a moment to individually notice and note celebrations and needs for our overall effectiveness. Remember, our goal for fiction is 90 percent and our overall goal is 85 percent.

Kathy: I'd like to start by celebrating our target two growth! Last cycle, this was at 74 percent, so twenty points is a testament to the work we've put in. What worked?

Angela: Most definitely the graphic organizer we designed based on our last common formative assessment data. Having the tool to connect the actions and interactions to the events in the plot was a game changer.

Lyndsay: I was worried that I spent too much time modeling how to use that organizer, but I could tell it was making such a difference in my small groups that I made it a daily check-in requirement as my classroom formative. I'm glad to see students were able to transfer that.

Martha: I want to also celebrate that we also had gains in target four. I've noticed that even as the text gets more complex, students are still working to go back to the plot elements to anchor what they're thinking. Annotating the text has been a huge help in ensuring they dig back into the text and cite evidence.

Kathy: Our students who are IEP eligible had success with that strategy, as well, especially with the text-to-speech accommodation that allows them to stop and take notes. I observed so many intentionally referencing their annotations during the assessment. That was evident when we were looking at individual student data. Now I'm thinking of how I can make that a part of the learning goal.

Lyndsay: So, it's funny because all of my general ed students did fine, but my special ed kids didn't.

Angela: Reset. Do you mean *our* students who are provided IEP services?

Lyndsay: Thank you, yes. Resetting that. Ours. I'm wondering what we need to learn to make sure our students that are provided IEP services are reaching level 3 proficiency. Maybe we can learn from Della?

Kathy: Della will be joining us at our next collaborative, so let's schedule twenty minutes on the agenda to pick her brain about additional practices we can implement. She can help us build some scaffolded text supports, too. Please note that on the minutes, and also, we'll need to bring student work samples. That needs to be an action item.

Martha: Done. And that naturally leads into what we've identified as a collective need.

Lyndsay: As a team, and I think largely because I need more support here, target one—analyzing the thoughts and motivations of a character—is a team need.

Angela: I think that we all were just dealing with so much coming back from our long weekend. The students were a little squirrelly, and the living history museum event that—

Kathy: Reset. Focus on what we can control.

Angela: Thank you. Resetting that. Yes. We've got work to do on target one. This wasn't a very complex plot structure, so I'm curious about what we can do here.

Martha: We spent so much time working through target two that we didn't realize analyzing thoughts and motivation would be an issue. I'm thinking back, and I did a lot of whole-group instruction here and didn't really focus on this in small-group instruction at all.

Angela: I'm now rethinking the excerpt I used for this. I don't think it was a great mentor text. And I rushed through target one to get to targets two and four, too. I think I overanticipated the struggle.

Kathy: I think this caught my attention too late. I didn't build a classroom quick check on this target because our class discussions were solid. It wasn't until closer to the end of the cycle that I checked again on a short text. I only had two days before our common formative assessment to clean it up, but that clearly wasn't enough time.

Lyndsay: I'm wondering now if that's what happened to me, as well. I didn't ask for any independent quick checks on target one. I integrated them into target two, so I didn't backtrack to the first step of the progression. Also, I didn't take the students beyond the plot summary frame.

Kathy: Let's note on our pacing document to revisit that. I can also model how I used response prompts to help students expand beyond the plot frame.

Martha: Good catch. Done!

Lyndsay: Yes, please! May we combine our morning classes for ten minutes and you lead students through the response prompts? And then I'd like to combine again in the afternoon, but I'll lead it this time, so you can provide me feedback.

Martha: And record it because I want to see it, too!

Angela: Same! Also, I'm glad we studied the assessment question stems before we built the common formative assessment, but I'm going to be completely transparent here. I had students reflect on those questions independently, but I never followed up. I moved straight to target two because I knew the question stems were more complex. I was anticipating the struggle.

Martha: I mean, they weren't complex, but did we miss how this is aligned with the author's purpose learning goal? Let's add that to our next agenda. We need to go back, rip open our end-of-year state assessment, and see what connections we can make there.

Kathy: Love it. And this is where I think we can calibrate some of our readers' response prompts. Let's bring the rubric for that, as well. Martha, will you note that on our agenda, too?

Martha: Done. Assigning Angela that step. OK?

Angela: Yup! I'll be ready.

Lyndsay: Oh, good! I need to hear how you all walk students through that tool.

Kathy: I'd like to bring us back to our overall team goals and targets. We are twelve percentage points away from our April goal. We will need to bring progress-monitoring data back from our intervention groups to make sure our plan is on track to help us meet our achievement goal. We revisit this standard on our unit assessment, so those data will be helpful, too.

Martha: All right, team. Our overall data reflection and action steps are set. Let's take another moment to reflect on our own professional effectiveness. Be ready to share one glow, grow, and go.

I'll go first. My glow is that I'm really proud of the readers' response prompts that I used for my quick checks. My grow is to refocus on analyzing characters. My go is to align my classroom assessments with the most rigorous question stems and work through connecting the character actions and thoughts to the bigger events in the plot structure.

Kathy: I'll go. My glow is the work that I've done with annotating text. My grow is to also get back to target one and ensure students are really understanding how characters move that plot along. My go is to restructure my small groups to embed target one and prep to model the prompt minilesson with Lyndsay.

Lyndsay: I'm going to start with my grow. I clearly need to re-engage students in more effective small-group instruction in target one and target four. My go is to revisit our graphic organizers and model annotating texts and work with Kathy on our plan. My glow is that even though I robbed Peter to pay Paul, my success with target two was directly because of the preparation I did because I knew it was going to be the most difficult target to teach.

Angela: My go is to gather more complex mentor texts. And I'm going to go back and look at my quick check prompts to see where the most common mistakes were because my grow is on target one, as well. My glow is the use of the graphic organizer that we created. Actually, that should be a team glow! I also have the action step to be prepared to walk the team through our rubric calibration.

Martha: All right, should we scan our agenda and see if there is anything we missed? Lyndsay, when ready, will you close us out?

Lyndsay: Our number-one question should be, How do we create champions for students?

Think back to the questions posed prior to both scenarios.

- Is the presence or absence of procedural norms and collective commitments evident in each scenario?

- How does each of the literacy teams approach comparing data?

- What markers are present to indicate a healthy or unhealthy data culture?

- Which literacy team is committed to engaging in collective inquiry and building shared expertise?

- Which team displays mutual accountability for shared literacy goals and professional effectiveness?

Both teams organize team agendas and utilize a team protocol for analyzing data. However, it's clear that the fifth-grade team has embraced the professional expectations of each member and used those expectations as an effective tool to guide the team's work. This is evident in the way the team members hold one another mutually accountable by using the term *reset* to bring the team's focus back to its shared agreements. In contrast, the third-grade team follows an agenda to organize its meeting, but if the team has established norms and commitments, they are not honored or present. Even with utilizing data analysis protocols, the two teams have very different approaches to comparing data. The third-grade team focuses on observing the data, while the fifth-grade team focuses on learning from the data. When it comes to establishing a healthy or unhealthy data culture, consider how the third-grade team spends its time complaining about student groups, wondering whether the test was too difficult, and analyzing the data by individual teachers' results. The complaining, the excuses, and the sense of *your data* over *our data* make this an example of what an unhealthy data discussion sounds like. Notice that the fifth-grade team dives into the results from the perspective of mutual accountability for shared goals. The team members approach the discussion through the lens of building shared knowledge to ensure they move students forward.

> Teams may be pros at disaggregating data by student by standard to determine, "How did *they* do?" but may not be as adept at analyzing the data by asking the question, "How did *we* do?"

While there is no doubt that the third-grade team members are pros at disaggregating data by student by standard to determine, "How did *they* do?" they are not as adept at analyzing the data by asking the question, "How did *we* do?" The fifth-grade team members ask the second question head-on. Through powerful collaborative discussion, they walk away with focused next steps for improved collective and individual practice. This takes intentionality, solid protocols, and purposeful practice.

TEAMS Process Protocol for Analyzing Data for Evidence of Instructional Effectiveness (Steps 6–10)

While accomplished literacy teams disaggregate data to learn more about how they can help students learn more, they also know the importance and value of intentionally celebrating what works. DuFour and colleagues (2016) note, "When celebrations continually remind people of the purpose and priorities of their organizations, members are more likely to embrace the purpose and work toward agreed-on priorities" (p. 221).

Celebrating progress and accomplishments, even in the smallest of increments, can build collective efficacy. Notice that in the fifth-grade team's conversation (page 98), team members align their celebrations with specific goals and instructional practices. Growth is celebrated as an achievement, but the conversation continues to center on reaching their shared goal. Teams need to create structures that ensure celebration is part of their collaborative data routines. Don't be stingy with naming and claiming what's going well *because of* your work!

> Celebrating progress and accomplishments, even in the smallest of increments, can build collective efficacy.

The following considerations will help literacy teams create or elevate team structures and collective practices to ensure data conversations lead to professional learning. Visit **go.SolutionTree.com/literacy** for a free reproducible version of this list.

- Have we established a clear purpose and focus for our data conversations?
- Have we collaboratively developed norms and collective commitments for data disaggregation?
- Do we align our data conversations with our SMART goal or team goal attainment?
- Are both individual teacher and collective teacher outcomes analyzed?
- Do we ask questions and engage in collective inquiry?
- Are we reliant on facts and evidence instead of opinions and assumptions?
- Is monitoring progress in our effectiveness part of our team's data routine?
- Have we included intentional and consistent opportunities to celebrate our work?

As with previous protocols, a summary of the steps follows.

- **Steps 6–10** ask teams to analyze the data to find strengths and note effective instructional practices, isolate areas of improvement, and determine what continued professional learning is needed to increase student achievement.

Continuing the work begun in chapter 3 (page 63), here are the last five steps of the protocol for analyzing data for evidence of instructional effectiveness, which also appear in the appendix A reproducible "TEAMS Process Protocol for Analyzing Data for Evidence of Instructional Effectiveness" (page 140). As we stated in previous chapters, this tool is not meant to be completed and turned in. We intend for it to guide rich conversations that lead to building shared knowledge.

1. **Name** the unit by genre or focus, and list the essential standards and learning targets that were assessed.

2. **Celebrate** reading data to determine overall gains and strengths as a grade level and for each class. All classes and students are accounted for.

3. **Discover** overall areas in need of continued support as a grade level and for each class. Ensure all classes and students are accounted for.

4. **Organize** support by student, by learning target, and by proficiency level (need).

5. **Plan** responses by determining which strategies will be most effective to respond when students do and do not learn.

6. **Claim** strengths, celebrations, or glows specific to literacy instructional practices both as a team and individually. Be generous and specific with celebrations!

7. **Target** areas of need, or grows, specific to literacy instructional practices both as a team and individually. Be intentional and specific when identifying needs.

8. **Learn** what professional learning or support is needed for improved literacy instructional practices both as a team and individually.

9. **Aim** to accomplish goals by aligning data outcomes with literacy SMART, team, or unit goal attainment.

10. **Commit** to actions and next steps to be implemented to meet individual and collective literacy instructional goals.

Figure 4.3 (page 106) provides a first-grade team's sample data for an essential foundational reading standard. Figure 4.4 (page 106) then shows what steps 6–10 of the protocol template might look like after the early literacy teacher team analyzes the data and records its reflections and discussions.

Team SMART goal: 96% at grade-level proficiency by May 20					
Team overall unit SMART goal: 85% at grade-level proficiency by November 20					
RF.1.3.E: Decode regularly spelled one-syllable words that follow syllable types (closed syllable, open syllable, vowel-consonant-e, vowel teams, consonant-le, and r-controlled vowel).					
Teacher	Learning Target One I can identify and say the five short vowel sounds.	Learning Target Two I can read CVC words with short vowel sounds.	Learning Target Three I can identify and say the five long vowel sounds.	Learning Target Four I can read open syllable words with long vowel sounds.	Overall
HG	98%	81%	100%	76%	88.75%
HP	87%	68%	98%	60%	78.25%
RW	98%	82%	100%	88%	92%
Team	94%	77%	98%	75%	86%

Source for standard: Arkansas Department of Education, n.d.

FIGURE 4.3: First-grade team data disaggregation sample.

6. **Claim** overall team strengths:	
Short vowel sounds have improved overall by 20% since September 1! Letter ID data are 100% in all vowels. Continued growth in letter-sound correspondence in short (+9%) and long vowels (+3%) met our overall unit goal! Woo-hoo!	
Individual Teacher Strengths	
HG	Letter ID and 15% gains in letter-sound correspondence since last progress check. Small-group instruction is targeted, and the new daily progress online tool I created has been huge in monitoring individual goals.
HP	The strongest area is in letter ID, and my focus on long vowel sounds using the visual anchors and flash cards showed 11 percentage points' growth. Using the musical sound cues is highly engaging.
RW	Students that are IEP entitled are all at 100% (independently without accommodations) in letter ID and sound correspondence because of the scaffolded accommodated chart we built with the specialist team.
7. **Target** overall team need: » Letter-sound correspondence with long vowels » Blending CVC » Decoding open syllable » Fluency	
Individual Teacher Needs	
HG	Target four (continue to progress monitor target two)

| HP | Target two / confusion of vowels /i/ and /e/ |
| RW | Target two / blending! |

8. **Learn** overall team professional learning or support needed:

» Strategies to blend and move beyond phoneme isolation in small-group instruction
» Engaging independent practice opportunities (not computer based) for open syllable

Individual Teacher Professional Learning or Support Needed

HG	Determining an effective way to transition practice from guided to independent; what's the right amount of teacher prompting and support?
HP	Need guidance and resources on how to help students differentiate between short vowels /i/ and /e/
RW	How to move students that are stuck on sounding out individual phonemes but not able to blend

9. **Aim** to achieve goals:

Did we meet our collective goal? Yes!

By what margin? +1.25%

What data do we need to collect to continue to monitor our SMART goal attainment?

Word list assessment, running records, progress-monitoring data, middle-of-the-year assessment data

How do these data impact upcoming unit goals?

Continue to grow the decoding to support upcoming blending and fluency unit goals. Focus on strategies that will accelerate students into more complex decoding skills.

10. **Commit** to next steps:

What actionable commitments do we make as a team?

» Each bring a strategy for blending to share at next collaborative (October 28).
» Bring student progress-monitoring word list assessments and running records for error analysis for next collaborative (October 28).
» Record five minutes of small group for feedback (due November 8).

Actionable Commitments We Make Individually

HG	Meet with literacy specialist to brainstorm ideas for transitions to independent practice, record my long vowel group for feedback, access district professional development notes from summer literacy training.
HP	Review teachers' manual and training kit for strategies for the tricky /i/ and /e/ vowels, observe Ronetta's classroom during whole group, collaboratively plan with team for upcoming interventions, email literacy specialist to model small group next week, record group for feedback.
RW	Access video series for phonics strategies, review word list assessment and running records, review training manual and kit materials, partner with kindergarten team on phonemic awareness strategies.

FIGURE 4.4: Analyzing data for evidence of instructional effectiveness protocol—Steps 6–10 example.

Data Don't Always Mean Numbers

Implementing and sustaining PLC practices hinges on teachers' collectively studying effective teaching and learning and investing in each other's professional growth. If teacher teams are going to achieve their enduring mission of ensuring all students learn at high levels, then they must commit to continuously deepening their knowledge to refine and elevate their craft. As we stated at the beginning of this chapter, teams must relentlessly study and purposefully celebrate data—the evidence of effectiveness—through the lens of collective inquiry.

> Teams must relentlessly study and purposefully celebrate data—the evidence of effectiveness—through the lens of collective inquiry.

The bulk of this chapter has been dedicated to the process of studying data after a common formative assessment, but collective inquiry does not go on hiatus between assessments. Reflective practitioners consider the variety of ways a team could analyze evidence of student learning in order to grow their practices on a daily basis lesson by lesson.

Data do not need to be collated and presented in a color-coded spreadsheet to learn from student work. A teacher who is having a hard time accelerating a student or group of students could bring the following to a team meeting.

- A few sample student reading responses
- A short video quickly taken on one's phone during a reading group
- Pictures of a student's phonics sort to analyze errors
- Anecdotal notes from a student reading conference

This and various other evidence would allow the teacher's teammates to understand where those students are on the path to proficiency and allow them to collaborate and share ideas about best practices that would help move the students forward while also building capacity in the teammate who shared.

For example, a first-grade team built capacity among the team members when one teacher brought student retelling graphs from a reading group that had strong phonics and fluency but was unable to retell with details from the text. The teacher showed the team how she had been using the retelling graph template in figure 4.5, with students coloring in one box for each event or detail included in their retelling (green for beginning of story, yellow for middle of story, or red for end of story). But over the course of two weeks, the students had not been able to meet their goal of retelling in sequence with details from the beginning, middle, and end of the story.

One teammate shared her experience that her students seemed to prioritize identifying the characters, setting, and problem in their retelling, but they skipped over key details. In response, she had created the detail dots tool shown in figure 4.6 (page 110) and printed it as bookmarks for students to use toward their retelling. Students were to pop a detail dot in the green bucket for each detail they included from the story's beginning, in the yellow for each detail from the middle, and in the red for each detail from the ending.

_____'s Retelling Graph

Source: ©2023 Mason Crest Elementary School. Adapted with permission.

FIGURE 4.5: Retelling graph template.

*Visit **go.SolutionTree.com/literacy** for a free reproducible version of this figure.*

Source: ©2023 Mason Crest Elementary School. Adapted with permission.

FIGURE 4.6: Detail dots tool.

*Visit **go.SolutionTree.com/literacy** for a free reproducible version of this figure.*

The special education teacher who supported this first-grade team and was part of the team's meetings shared that her students improved their retelling when she made it into a game board (shown in figure 4.7) that they wanted to play with after every book they read independently or read aloud together. They each moved their playing piece from the first space to each successive spot on the board by saying the connecting word they landed on, followed by the next event or detail in the story, and tried to include enough details in their retelling so that they could get all the way around the board.

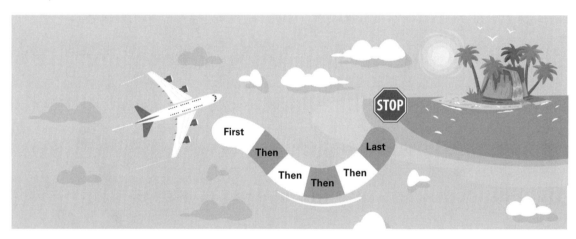

Source: ©2023 Mason Crest Elementary School. Adapted with permission.

FIGURE 4.7: Sequencing stories game board.

*Visit **go.SolutionTree.com/literacy** for a free reproducible version of this figure.*

The last two teammates mentioned here had evidence of the effectiveness of these strategies from using them in their own classes and gave their teammate a new tool to try to improve her students' evidence of learning. She did not have to wait until the common formative assessment to share her emerging evidence that this group of students was not making expected progress. It is true collective responsibility when teammates ensure teaching and learning will improve each week because each one of them has a seat at the table and uses collaborative time to focus on the right work. That work includes analyzing evidence that leads to better individual and collective practices and higher student reading achievement.

Get Going or Get Better

As you think about your systems and structures to support literacy teams in ensuring that all students are reading at high levels, what changes, refinements, or complete overhauls would help teams purposefully celebrate data and collaboratively analyze data for evidence of effectiveness of individual and collective teacher practices? Use the reproducible "Get Going on Chapter 4: Measure Effectiveness of Individual and Collective Teacher Practices" (page 112) as a reflection tool for the learning in chapter 4 to move forward in the collaborative work of literacy teams.

Get Going on Chapter 4:
Measure Effectiveness of Individual and
Collective Teacher Practices

» Does your team prioritize analyzing data through the lens of professional learning and evaluating collective and individual instructional practices?

» Has your team aligned data outcomes with SMART, team, or unit goals?

» Are protocols, norms, and collective commitments in place to create a healthy data culture?

» Does the team intentionally celebrate effective individual and collective instructional practices?

Getting Started?	Getting Better?
Providing opportunities to practice data vulnerability is a great way to get started. Be sure to review norms and collective commitments to ensure healthy data discussions. If teachers have never shared their data before, then before a first data discussion, you may want to remove the personal element by starting with fake data with made-up names. Assign each team member to represent one of the fictional teachers and practice using the protocol provided. Reflect on where the team had strengths and vulnerabilities, and refine norms if necessary. Another option is to include real data but remove teacher names this first time, keeping in mind that teachers may need to get comfortable being uncomfortable in order to move on to real data aligned with real teachers.	If your team is already discussing data, not just to group students or adjust instruction but to gather evidence of professional effectiveness, then consider how you are using data as a tool to determine areas of professional growth. If the team or each teacher creates a professional SMART goal centered on improving instructional practices in literacy, then each data discussion also becomes an opportunity to support each teacher in attaining an individual or collective SMART goal. As the collaborative team members share data, their transparency of practice becomes more purposeful as their insights, guidance, support, or resources move them toward reaching their goals. Teams that are engaged in this level of goal-prioritized practice operate under the mantra, *No one learns alone.*

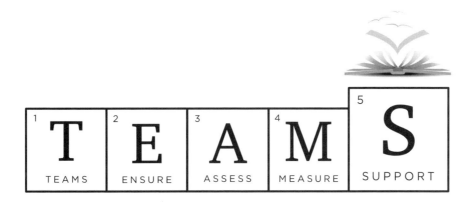

1	2	3	4	5
T	E	A	M	S
TEAMS	ENSURE	ASSESS	MEASURE	SUPPORT

Support Systematically With Targeted Acceleration, Interventions, and Extensions

One of our favorite quotes from Richard DuFour (2015), which comes from his book *In Praise of American Educators: And How They Can Become Even Better*, is, "If there is one undeniable reality for every educator every year, it is that we are going to work hard. The real question is this: Will we work hard and succeed or work hard and fail?" (p. 252). We would argue that if your literacy team has engaged in the work detailed in the previous four chapters, then you most certainly have worked hard and—based on the results at schools we've worked with—you are succeeding for more students than you did before having these protocols and processes to guide you to the right work.

In the previous chapter, you learned how to have deeply productive data discussions that improve your individual and collective practices and lead to higher levels of literacy for students, especially those who were not yet proficient when the data were collected. We now address how to plan for, implement, and monitor the progress of the interventions and extensions your team develops because of those data discussions.

We want to make it abundantly clear that even though this is the last chapter of the book, literacy teams do not wait until this point in the process to systematically respond to learning. They do that not only *after* reading assessments but also as part of strong, differentiated Tier 1 core instruction in every classroom from the beginning of the unit. Our focus now shifts to answering critical questions three and four as your literacy team creates a plan for additional time and support for students who are not proficient at the end of the unit and need *further* systematic interventions or students who are ready to be extended beyond the grade-level reading expectation. The S in TEAMS stands for *support*, but *systematically* is an equally crucial S. Many schools provide interventions, but students somehow fall through the cracks because of scheduling, limited resources, or interventions that are left up to the individual classroom teacher to figure out. The key to ensuring learning for all is creating a system that guarantees every student who needs additional time and support receives it, no matter what.

In this chapter, intervention as part of the teaching-assessing cycle is covered, as is individual student intervention progress monitoring. You will get a step-by-step protocol to intervention progress monitoring, in addition to a look at communication and collaboration around intervention, reassessment, and regrouping, and systems of intervention and extension. This chapter also includes the reproducible "Get Going on Chapter 5: Support Systematically With Targeted Acceleration, Interventions, and Extensions" (page 133). The focus of the chapter is how teams support and extend systematically with targeted acceleration, interventions, and extensions to meet all students' needs, the last of the five tight elements of teaching reading in a PLC.

WORD STUDY

> **systematically** *adverb* [si-stə-ˈma-ti-k(ə-)lē] According to a fixed plan or system; marked by thoroughness and regularity; methodically (Systematically, n.d.)

Intervention as Part of the Teaching-Assessing Cycle

To create a schoolwide system of interventions, certain actions must be done at the school level rather than the team level. These actions include scheduling time and resources in the master calendar, establishing a timely process for intervention identification, and coordinating interventions for students needing both academic and behavioral supports (Buffum, Mattos, & Malone, 2018). However, in this chapter, as we have done throughout this book, we focus on what the *team* can control, which is creating a plan based on the reading data to meet the needs of each student requiring additional time and support, and then monitoring the progress of the learning happening in small-group reading intervention.

Many schools and districts use tiered instruction in a response to intervention (RTI) process, with new grade-level instruction happening in Tier 1 and additional time and support being given to students in Tiers 2 and 3. Small-group reading instruction should occur during all tiers of instruction. When we target student needs in small groups during Tier 1 core instruction, we refer to that as *prevention*. Then, after the end-of-unit assessment, when the focus of instruction moves on to a new unit, students who still need additional time and support to become proficient on the grade-level essential standard will receive support in Tier 2, which we refer to as *intervention*. A few students may concurrently receive individual Tier 3 support to fill in gaps in below-grade-level foundational skills; this is often referred to as *remediation* (Buffum et al., 2018).

We would like to replace the term *remediation* with *acceleration*. It's important to reframe the language to ensure its connotation implies moving students forward. We make those distinctions between prevention, intervention, and acceleration in order to be clear that the process we introduce in this chapter is what teams go through when systematically identifying and monitoring students' progress in Tier 2 reading interventions.

WORD STUDY

acceleration *noun* [ik-ˌse-lə-ˈrā-shən] The act or process of moving faster or happening more quickly (Acceleration, n.d.)

intervention *noun* [in-tər-ˈven(t)-shən] Action taken to have an effect on its outcome and improve a situation (Intervention, n.d.)

prevention *noun* [pri-ˈven(t)-shən] The act of stopping something from happening or arising (Prevention, n.d.)

Figure 5.1 (page 116) shows the teaching-assessing cycle from *Taking Action: A Handbook for RTI at Work* (Buffum et al., 2018), which is a tremendous resource if your team needs further understanding and clarification on the RTI at Work process. As you can see, we have given the specific TEAMS process protocols from chapters 2, 3, and 4 to address three of the four corners of that cycle as we answer the critical questions of learning in the PLC at Work process. If our mission is high levels of learning for *all* and we know that not all students learn at the same rate or same time, then we now need a process for teams to address students who need reading intervention in Tier 2 in order to complete the cycle.

The more targeted the intervention, the more likely it is to succeed (Buffum, Mattos, & Weber, 2010). When teams give an end-of-unit assessment and find that some students are not yet proficient in the essential standard, then it is clear which students need intervention and what the specific target will be. However, some schools have reading intervention groups for students currently reading below grade level, and often, students stay reading below grade level because those interventions are not targeted to the specific student's need. Think back to figure 2.1 (page 36), which illustrates reading's critical components: phonemic awareness, phonics, fluency, vocabulary, and comprehension, on a foundation of oral language. Be sure that any reading intervention groups happening are designed to target student skills in one specific area instead of just addressing struggling readers.

> Be sure that any reading intervention groups happening are designed to target student skills in one specific area instead of just addressing struggling readers.

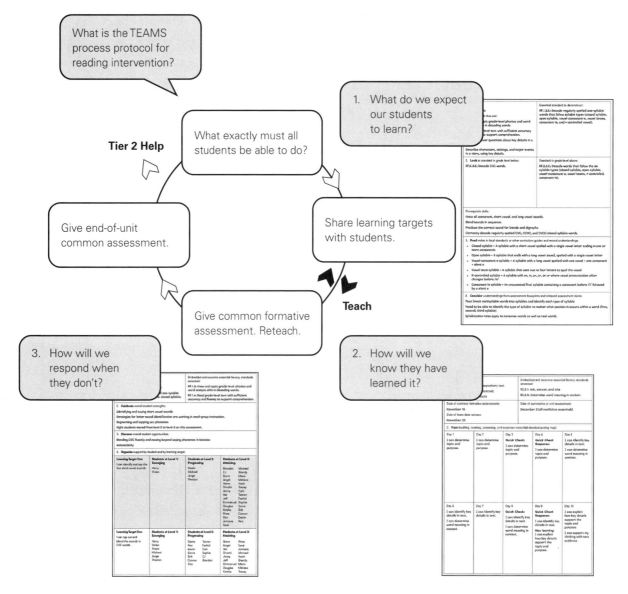

Source: Buffum, Mattos, & Malone, 2018; Buffum, Mattos, & Weber, 2012.

FIGURE 5.1: How each of the TEAMS process protocols aligns with the teaching-assessing cycle.

Jacquie learned this lesson the hard way as a finance major who discovered the business world wasn't for her and decided to use her love of numbers to teach middle school mathematics. When her first teaching job ended up being in a fourth-grade classroom, she loved teaching fractions and long division, but didn't know how to help the students who came to her class reading below grade level. She called them *low readers*, as did all the other teachers she worked with. The students' parents were told their students needed to read more to get caught up.

If Jacquie could find those first students, who are now adults, she would apologize to them because when you know better, you do better. Instead, we teachers can make amends by realizing our language shapes our thoughts and holding ourselves and our colleagues accountable for using language that shows we have high expectations for all. When thinking about your reading groups, stop yourself and your teammates from thinking *my high group* and *my low group* or, even worse, *my low babies*, as it can affect student achievement (Chang, 2011; Jacobs, 2020; Rosenthal & Jacobson, 1968). Instead of labeling students as *low*, label the skill that reading group needs to work on. If you cannot identify which specific skills a group of students currently reading below grade level needs in order to improve, that is more a reflection of your teaching practices than of the students' capabilities. Students are not *low*. They are learners. They need you to label the skill you will teach them, not them as people. How about *my fluency group* or *my comprehension group*? Even better, refer to each group by its goal, such as *my twenty-five sight words group, my phrased and fluent group,* or *my central message comprehension group.*

> Students are not *low*. They are learners. They need you to label the skill you will teach them, not them as people.

Individual Student Intervention Progress Monitoring

If your team has had a data discussion after an end-of-unit assessment, then the decision for which specific area of reading you'll target in your intervention groups has already been made. (For example, chapter 4's sample data discussion about main idea—see figure 4.3, page 106—would target comprehension, and the sample data analysis protocol on long vowel sounds would target phonics—see figure 4.4, page 106.) However, if you currently have reading intervention groups for your students reading below grade level but those groups are not as targeted as they need to be, you could target each student's needs as shown in figure 5.2. This figure includes identifying the students' strengths to build on and the specific component of reading to address for each student reading below grade level. You could then regroup students by identified need and make a plan to better address those needs in intervention groups based on the components of reading.

Student name: Jairo R.		Date: End of first quarter	
Reading Data Strengths and Needs	**Intervention Action Steps**	**Person Responsible, Timing, and Ratio**	**Data Collection and Reassessment Date**
Oral Language Strong communication skills and emerging academic language	NA	NA	NA
Phonemic Awareness On grade level	NA	NA	NA

FIGURE 5.2: Systematically monitoring individual student reading progress.

continued ▶

Reading Data Strengths and Needs	Intervention Action Steps	Person Responsible, Timing, and Ratio	Data Collection and Reassessment Date
Phonics On grade level	NA	NA	NA
Fluency Level 20 32 words per minute Reads at good rate but omits words without self-correction	monitor in Tier I reading group.	NA	Running record
Vocabulary In content areas but not from books	monitor in Tier I reading group.	NA	Retelling rubric
Comprehension District assessment 63% Can answer literal questions but not higher level and needs work on retelling with details	Have intervention group three times per week for four weeks.	Butler's inference group Monday, Wednesday, and Friday rotation two 1:4 teacher-to-student ratio	Retelling rubric and inference open response with evidence from text in three weeks

TEAMS Process Protocol for Monitoring Intervention Progress

Whether your team is forming intervention groups after a specific assessment or analyzing the strengths and needs of readers as shown in figure 5.2 (page 117), it is crucial to get individual students the interventions they each need. We have developed a step-by-step protocol to take you from that first identification of needs all the way through implementing the interventions, reassessing to determine if the interventions were successful, and determining new needs.

Here is a brief summary of the steps.

- **Steps 1–3** ask teams to decide what intervention groups they will form, which students best fit into each group, which teacher best fits to lead the learning of each group, and how to make sure the students, teachers, and time all fit into their intervention schedule.

- **Steps 4–6** ask teams to set a specific goal for what students in each intervention group will be able to do after a specified period of time, and to decide what assessment they will use to reassess and measure the effectiveness of the intervention and the growth in student reading progress.

- **Steps 7–10** ask teams to clarify how they will plan for, as well as collaborate and communicate about, the learning in intervention groups with all adults who work with each student. This way, everyone is on the same page, and the learning from the intervention can be transferred to and reinforced in the classroom. Either the student makes enough progress to no longer need the intervention or, after reassessing, the team members realize they need to change course and make the intervention more intense to get the desired results.

As your team begins the process of creating a system of interventions, we've provided examples that outline how it might look when you create targeted intervention groups with specific goals and a timeline for reassessment as these teams did. In both cases, the teams completed the first six steps—given here—in the process of intervention progress monitoring to launch targeted intervention groups. (Steps 7–10 are discussed in later sections of this chapter.) The steps to the protocol also appear in appendix A as the reproducible "TEAMS Process Protocol for Monitoring Intervention Progress" (page 141).

1. **Analyze** students' current strengths and needs.
2. **Determine** the focus-of-intervention area and action steps needed.
3. **Decide** who will meet those needs and when the groups fit in the schedule.
4. **Establish** data collection and reassessment measures and dates.
5. **Create** a short-term SMART goal for each intervention group.
6. **Set** the next date for progress monitoring to determine if the goal was met for each student.
7. **Clarify** what all adults working with the student are expected to communicate and in what format they should communicate it.
8. **Plan** targeted lessons with built-in opportunities to collaborate around learning.
9. **Reassess** and monitor progress to determine if the goal was met.
10. **Regroup** for instruction on a new goal, or increase the intensity of intervention.

Figure 5.3 shows how a third-grade team analyzed the strengths and needs of students in its current ineffective intervention groups. The team regrouped for more targeted interventions that specified which component of reading each group would focus on and what text level each group would use. And for the first time, the team used *I can* statements to set goals for each group, and the team set dates when it would reassess and determine if each student had met the goal and could be discontinued from the intervention or needed more time and support. See appendix B for the reproducible "Targeted Intervention Groups and Goals Template" (page 156).

Students in Intervention Group	Classroom Teacher	Intervention Action Steps	Reading Skill Goal	Group Teacher, Timing, and Ratio	Data Collection and Reassessment Date
Mark M. Karyl L. Allie A.	Deinhart Freese Barrett	Phonics and fluency in mid-fourth-grade text	I can decode multisyllable words to read fluently.	Barrett Monday, Wednesday, and Friday Rotation one 1:3	Decoding assessment and running record Three weeks
Griffith C. Tessa G. Tommy H. Nicholas P.	Freese Butler Deinhart Butler	Comprehension by scaffolding early fifth-grade text	I can explain how characters' actions affect plot.	Deinhart Monday and Wednesday Rotation two 1:4	Comprehension rubric Two weeks
Emmie M. Deacon D. Zoey G. Jake M.	Deinhart Deinhart Barrett Freese	Fluency by scaffolding beginning fourth-grade text	I can group words into phrases to read fluently.	Freese Monday, Wednesday, and Friday Rotation two 1:4	Running record audio recording Two weeks

Source for standard: NGA & CCSSO, 2010.

FIGURE 5.3: Targeted intervention groups and goals template used to record needs in students receiving reading intervention—First assessment.

Figure 5.4 shows the same team later in the year, after they have used our step-by-step protocol for responding to evidence of learning. They have had the data discussion you read in the previous chapter after their assessment on the essential standard and created short-term intervention groups based on those data. These groups are all moving students forward in their comprehension skills but working on different rungs of the learning progression ladder by focusing on one specific learning target rather than the overall standard.

Students in Intervention Group	Classroom Teacher	Intervention Action Steps	Reading Skill Goal	Group Teacher, Timing, and Ratio	Data Collection and Reassessment Date
Casey A. Henry G. Emily F. Claire R.	Deinhart Freese Barrett Barrett	TEKS 5.3B Learning target one in fourth-grade text	I can analyze the relationships and conflicts of characters.	Barrett February 18–20 1:4	Questions 1–4 February 21
Matt T. Taylor W. Anisa B. Lyndsay R. Cheryl K.	Freese Butler Deinhart Butler Butler	TEKS 5.3B Learning target three by scaffolding fifth-grade text	I can compare and contrast characters within stories.	Butler February 18–20 1:5	Questions 3 and 4 February 21
Amy H. Chris J. Martha C. Kelli F. Katie A.	Deinhart Deinhart Barrett Freese Freese	RL.5.3 Learning target four in grade-level text	I can infer meaning from text and quote textual evidence to support my thinking.	Freese February 18–20 1:5	Questions 3–6 February 21

Source for standard: Texas Education Agency, n.d.

FIGURE 5.4: Targeted intervention groups and goals template used to record needs in students receiving reading intervention—Summative assessment.

Communication and Collaboration About Interventions

As you can see in figures 5.3 and 5.4, often the person leading the intervention group is not the student's classroom teacher. While a system of interventions and extensions can be created that keeps students contained in their classroom, it is much more efficient to group students with like needs across classes. That means having at least two teachers working on reading goals with these students.

Keep in mind these are the students who did not easily reach proficiency the first time they were exposed to the skill or strategy, so sometimes it is incredibly beneficial for them to hear it presented in a different way from a different voice. But sometimes it can also be detrimental and confusing if a student has burgeoning understanding and then hears different instructional language. For example, Jacquie led intervention groups for kindergartners learning letters and sounds and developed a habit of referring to *big, tall, capital, uppercase letters* because some of the classroom teachers called them *big-little letters*, while another kindergarten teacher called them *uppercase-lowercase letters*, and the assessment referred to them as *capital letters*. We cannot expect students with emerging knowledge of a skill or strategy to have the flexibility to be able to interpret differences in our instructional language, so it is critical that the adults take on the responsibility of communicating about the learning happening in interventions and back in the classroom.

If each intervention group has an electronic form such as that in figure 5.5, then both the person leading the intervention and the classroom teacher have easy access to jot notes about the learning or share particular strategies, prompts, or tips that worked with certain students. Or both people can deposit questions to bring to the team during their collaborative time later in the week if they need something clarified or want support moving forward with the group or individual student. This is how your team can address the next two steps in the process of intervention progress monitoring. See appendix B for the reproducible "Communicating and Collaborating About Learning in Interventions Template" (page 157).

Reading Group Goal	Focus of Instruction (Learning Target)	Strategies to Share or Questions for Team
Decode one-syllable CVC words.	Blending sounds in sequence (using tools, then fingers, then no scaffold)	Successful blending with sound boxes and word tiles, but two students don't have the fine motor dexterity to tap out sounds on fingers, so keep trying or switch strategies?
Student Name	**Notes From Intervention**	**Notes From Classroom**
mursal	Absent from intervention group for two days	NA
Braxton	Strong letter-sound knowledge but difficulty coordinating the tapping on fingers	Has trouble with other fine motor tasks like cutting, so needs to build finger strength
Oumar	Taps backward, so working on coordinating thumb to index finger first; not yet able to blend sounds	Had him tap on desk instead of tap thumb to finger, and that seemed to work better for him
maxine	Huge progress! Can blend without tools	Great news but not yet seeing that transfer to classroom

FIGURE 5.5: Systematically communicating and collaborating about learning in interventions.

The following steps show the TEAMS process protocol for intervention progress monitoring. Steps 1–6 were discussed earlier (page 118), and now, we will focus on steps 7 and 8. We visit steps 9 and 10 later in this chapter, in the section Reassessment and Regrouping (page 126).

1. **Analyze** students' current strengths and needs.

2. **Determine** the focus-of-intervention area and action steps needed.

3. **Decide** who will meet those needs and when the groups fit in the schedule.

4. **Establish** data collection and reassessment measures and dates.

5. **Create** a short-term SMART goal for each intervention group.

6. **Set** the next date for progress monitoring to determine if the goal was met for each student.

7. **Clarify** what all adults working with the student are expected to communicate and in what format they should communicate it.

8. **Plan** targeted lessons with built-in opportunities to collaborate around learning.

9. **Reassess** and monitor progress to determine if the goal was met.

10. **Regroup** for instruction on a new goal, or increase the intensity of intervention.

After the team has formed intervention groups and clarified what is expected to be communicated among all adults working with those students, it is time to plan targeted lessons. Depending on your district's curriculum, your lesson-planning format, the time available for small-group instruction, and how your master schedule looks, those lessons will look different, but you can improve them by continuing to collaborate and share ideas across the team. Often, we teach something the best we know how the first time around, and when it comes time to do an intervention, we have no tools left at our disposal, yet we know just saying it slower and louder will not be effective.

The completed example in figure 5.6 (page 124) illustrates how teams could approach this work target by target, addressing essential conversations of critical question three during their collaborative time so teachers each have ideas to apply to their intervention group plans. See appendix B for the reproducible "Building a Response Plan by Learning Target: Critical Question Three (Grow)" (page 158).

Some districts have purchased curricula that teams must use. It is important to note there is a difference between *doing* a curriculum and *using* a curriculum. Simply doing every learning task provided and giving equal weight and time to every lesson in the curriculum goes against the first big idea of a PLC of focusing on learning over teaching.

The goal is not to simply *cover* every lesson, but to *use* the curriculum to help your students *learn* what your data show they need. Many purchased curricula specify which standards their lessons address, but it is up to the literacy team to determine where those lessons fit in the

Unit:
Decoding short and long vowel sounds
Essential Literacy Standard:
RF.I.3.E—Decode regularly spelled one-syllable words that follow syllable types (closed syllable, open syllable, vowel-consonant-e, vowel teams, consonant-le, and r-controlled vowel).

Learning Target		Question Three: Grow	Team Notes
I can identify and say the five short vowel sounds.	➡	**What intervention strategies are most effective?**	Hand motions for each short vowel sound, visual cue flash cards, say-see-trace, short vowel scavenger hunt
I can tap out and blend the sounds in CVC words.	➡	**What intervention strategies are most effective?**	Sound boxes, tap and slide, word tiles, magic reveal with index card or wand, push-up sounds
I can read CVC words with short vowel sounds.	➡	**What intervention strategies are most effective?**	Blending with slide decks, decodable text, flip-up chart word building and reading, word detective in non-decodable text
I can identify and say the five long vowel sounds.	➡	**What intervention strategies are most effective?**	Hand motions for each long vowel sound, visual cue flash cards, say-see-trace, long vowel scavenger hunt
I can read open syllable words with long vowel sounds.	➡	**What intervention strategies are most effective?**	Blending with slide decks, decodable text, phoneme deletion flip chart, word detective in non-decodable text

Source for standard: Texas Education Agency, n.d.

FIGURE 5.6: First-grade team example of building a response plan by learning target—Critical question three (grow).

learning progression of specific learning targets they have created. Figure 5.7 is a tool teams can use to collectively review their purchased curricula to determine which aspects of which lessons give students the best opportunities to become proficient on the specific learning targets they need to practice.

Unit:	Start Date:	End Date:
Essential Standard:	Essential Standard:	Essential Standard:
Learning Targets (*number*):	Learning Targets (*number*):	Learning Targets (*number*):
Pacing and Alignment of Curricula With Essential Standards' Learning Targets		
Lessons From Purchased Curricula:	Learning Targets Addressed by Lesson:	Team Adaptations to Provide More Targeted Opportunities:

FIGURE 5.7: Purchased curricula alignment tool.

*Visit **go.SolutionTree.com/literacy** for a free reproducible version of this figure.*

As both the classroom teacher and the intervention teacher plan their individual lessons, they will use the best resources available to them. However, we are often asked if they should be using grade-level or below-grade-level texts with students who need intervention. As you think about your lessons, it makes sense that your team uses grade-level text resources during Tier 1 instruction, but teachers often go straight to below-grade-level text in intervention because they believe the data show students were unable to apply the skill being taught in grade-level text. Because texts change in picture support, grammar, structure, clarity of language, and knowledge demands as the level of text complexity increases, teachers cannot assume that a student who can apply a skill in a below-grade-level text will eventually be able to do it in a grade-level text.

While below-grade-level texts are used in Tier 3 acceleration, figure 5.8 (page 126) shows that the planned Tier 2 intervention groups should consider how the teacher leading the intervention may need to scaffold the grade-level text in order for students to successfully apply their emerging skill. For example, if an intervention group is working on a comprehension skill of identifying main idea and details, the intervention teacher may need to preview the vocabulary and scaffold for students struggling to decode the text due to their phonics skills. That way, the students can access the grade-level text to work on main idea and details.

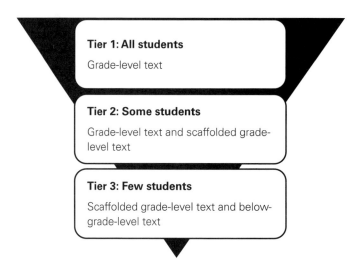

Source: Adapted from Buffum et al., 2018.

FIGURE 5.8: Matching text to need in small-group instruction in Tiers 1, 2, and 3.

Reassessment and Regrouping

Once the students are in targeted groups and the teachers are communicating, collaborating, and planning lessons with appropriate resources, you should begin to see progress. Teachers should regularly do quick checks (every few lessons) so that as soon as any student demonstrates proficiency in the skill, that student can be dismissed from the group, and the teacher leading the intervention can better focus on the students in need. When there is no longer a need, there is no longer an intervention.

> Students do not need to retake an entire summative assessment such as the one that was analyzed to initially make the intervention groups, because each group focused on a specific learning target.

Literacy teams often wonder if they have to create a whole new assessment or if students should retake the initial assessment after receiving additional time and support in intervention to determine whether the students have made progress in the targeted skill. There are many options, but the team should determine how they will reassess before the interventions begin so everyone is clear on the end goal. Sometimes teachers' anecdotal notes from the intervention group sessions can be enough evidence to determine if students can be discontinued, but often it is more objective to have students perform a task or answer questions on a short assessment. Students do not need to retake an entire summative assessment such as the one that was analyzed to initially make the intervention groups, because each group focused on a specific learning target. Therefore, each group only needs to answer questions or perform tasks related to that specific learning target. If you refer back to the last column of figure 5.4 (page 121), you can see this team did choose to create a new assessment with six questions about a passage. But one group only needed to answer questions 3 and 4 to show if they could compare and contrast characters, while another group answered questions 1–4 to show if they had met their goal and could now analyze characters.

After the reassessment, students may be discontinued from needing further intervention, or some students may need to be regrouped for additional targeted instruction based on the reassessment data. If students did not make expected progress during the intervention, then you cannot just continue to do the same thing, so figure 5.9 shows adaptations to consider that would increase the intensity of the intervention.

Intervention Consideration	Questions Teams Ask After Reassessment to Increase Intervention Intensity and Effectiveness
Frequency	Do the students need more reading group sessions per week to develop the skill?
	Are they only working on the skill during the intervention group, or is it being reinforced by the classroom teacher during reading?
Duration	Do the students need a longer reading group time in order to get both instruction and guided practice of the skill?
	Do they need a shorter reading group time because we are asking them to work intensely at difficulty for longer than they can handle?
Ratio	Do the students need a smaller student-to-teacher ratio in the reading group?
	Are the specific student dispositions in the group counterproductive to accelerating individual reading skills, meaning these students should be regrouped?
Targeted	Is there a clear SMART goal for the reading group, and is it the priority skill for this student to develop as a reader at this time?
	Have we examined the reason for the lack of proficiency (skill or will) and grouped students with the same need to target why they are not yet proficient?
Expertise	Is the person leading the intervention the best match for the skill and the student disposition?
	Are we sharing and learning from those who have gotten better results?

FIGURE 5.9: Five considerations to systematically make reading intervention more intense.

If you have students who are not initially successful in interventions, then be sure your team asks these questions and changes your response before throwing up your hands and proclaiming, "We've tried everything. These students need to be tested for special education." As our colleagues and special education experts Megan Clarke and Kristen Bordonaro (2022) state, "If your staff isn't fighting harder to keep students *out* of special education than they are fighting to get them in, you're doing it wrong."

Systems of Intervention and Extension

You now have a great deal to think about and new tools to use as you determine what students must know and be able to do (PLC critical question one; know), how you will know if they have learned it (PLC critical question two; show), and how you will respond when learning does not occur (PLC critical question three; grow). The oft-overlooked fourth and final question asks your team to consider how you will extend those students who are already proficient (glow) because every student must make at least a year's worth of academic gains in any given school year, or you do not have high levels of learning for all. Too often, it taxes all our time, effort, and resources to address the needs of those students reading below grade level, and the best we can manage for those reading above grade level is to let them choose a book of higher text complexity and give them time to read while we work with other students. We can do better.

Let's first clarify what it means to extend learning. *Extension* is sometimes confused with acceleration or enrichment. *Enrichment* may mean going into more depth, breadth, and complexity on a standard or skill. But it is also frequently used to describe incorporating visual or performing arts, cultural activities, or technology into instruction, which may not necessarily extend the learning but might be an enjoyable learning task once the required learning is achieved. *Extension* refers to the differentiated lessons that address the needs of those students already proficient in the essential standard by applying the skill in more complex text or dipping into the rigor expected at the next grade level's standard.

WORD STUDY

enrichment *noun* [in-ʹrich-mənt] The action of improving or enhancing the quality of something (Enrichment, n.d.)

extension *noun* [ik-ʹsten(t)-shən] An enlargement in scope or operation (Extension, n.d.)

How to reteach those students needing additional time and support is often more obvious to teachers than how they might extend the learning for those already proficient. Therefore, during a literacy team's collaborative time, it is important to address this target by target and brainstorm options. The completed example in figure 5.10 illustrates how teams would approach this work target by target, addressing essential conversations of critical question four. See appendix B for the reproducible "Building a Response Plan by Learning Target: Critical Question Four (Glow)" (page 159).

Paula coached a literacy team that wanted to develop a deeper understanding of how to effectively respond to the multiple layers in a continuum of proficiency. As the team answered critical question three, they identified students just beginning to develop skills and understanding as requiring intensive supports at proficiency level 1, and those progressing but not yet at grade-level expectations as needing acceleration at proficiency level 2. They then answered critical question four for students who were at proficiency level 3, who had met the expectations and were in need of extended learning that stretched them beyond grade level. To address each level of need, Paula created a sample response plan for the team to study (shown in figure 5.11, page 130) that included both students who needed interventions and students who needed extensions.

Can you imagine being a new teacher or changing grade levels and landing on a team that has dug so deeply into the content in this way that it has a common plan not only for teaching and assessing the essential standards but also for providing both interventions and extensions around those standards so that you can accomplish the mission of high levels of learning for all?

Unit:			
Fiction unit two			

Essential Literacy Standard:

TEKS 5.3B—Analyze the relationships of and conflicts among the characters.

Learning Target		Question Four: Glow	Team Notes
I can identify essential characters.	→	**What extension strategies will deepen the learning?**	Using familiar text, students determine which characters could be removed from the story without changing the plot; using short story text, students swap essential characters and rewrite with the new character in place.
I can analyze characters' thoughts, actions, and motivations.	→	**What extension strategies will deepen the learning?**	Students match dialogue to plot events using *if–then* prompts for characters' actions and reactions, and *what if?* prompts; if character reactions had been different, how would other characters have responded?
I can analyze the relationships and conflicts of characters.	→	**What extension strategies will deepen the learning?**	Students use the "But Why?" graphic organizer, linking dialogue to examine the relationships and conflicts of characters within the text, and add thought bubbles for subtext; students explain what other actions might have occurred if a different character experienced an event or if characters swapped places.
I can compare and contrast characters, ideas, and events within stories.	→	**What extension strategies will deepen the learning?**	Students choose characters from two texts and find text evidence to match various emotions and reactions; they connect theme to each character.

Source for standard: Texas Education Agency, n.d.

FIGURE 5.10: Fifth-grade team example of building a response plan by learning target—Critical question four (glow).

When we educators embrace this work, we are able to reflect on DuFour's (2015) quote that opened this chapter and answer his question confidently: "If there is one undeniable reality for every educator every year, it is that we are going to work hard. The real question is this: Will we work hard and succeed or work hard and fail?" (p. 252). We can succeed for more students than we are currently. We must respond as if students' lives depend on it, because now more than ever, in more ways than we even know, they do.

Now *that's* a reading war we're willing to fight.

Learning Target	Intensive (Emerging)	Accelerating (Progressing)	Extending (Exceeding)
I can identify the main topic.	Teachers provide sentence stems and visual support across multiple titles and short text in high-interest topics or familiar text. Teachers provide (explicitly state) an example and non-example of main idea statements for multiple texts. Students determine which main idea statement is a match.	After shared reading, the student reads text in isolation that is the topic statement and additional text that includes detail statements. Students identify the topic statement from the mentor text.	Students read more complex text and can identify the main idea or topic by writing a main idea statement that includes both topic and purpose. Students collaborate to determine alignment with text.
I can determine the purpose of the text.	Teachers create a sorting element that matches the general purpose of the text. Follow with a sentence stem or framework for students to have specific details that describe the purpose.	Students determine the purpose from discriminating from a bank of appropriate choices with familiar text. The student reads new text (access provided when needed) and applies the same discrimination from text with unfamiliar reads.	Students determine the purpose with a variety of unfamiliar texts (access provided when needed). Students create a comparison chart of text purposes across multiple familiar texts.
I can identify key details in a text.	Teachers provide a graphic organizer with boxes that do and do not support the main idea statement. Students separate the details that do not support the main idea and write in the details that do support the main idea.	Students complete the main idea and key details graphic organizer that requires students to choose statements from text that represent both key and supporting details. Only the key details make the graphic organizer.	Students complete the main idea and key details graphic organizer for their own informational topic of choice. Students compare a book or text on their topic to their own graphic organizer.
I can retell key details of a text.	Teachers reference work from the learning target of identifying key details. Use a mentor text and framework for retelling familiar text. Teachers determine key details in text boxes or other graphic organizers that state the main idea. Use the graphic organizer to prompt students through formal verbal or written retelling. Utilizing pictures or icon cards with text to organize key details with main idea topic statements, students use sentence frames and vocabulary support from text to write or verbally state the identified key details. Students apply all the scaffolded supports with new text. Reading support for grade-level text access is provided.	Utilizing a graphic organizer for the main idea in familiar texts, students share key details verbally. Students determine key details in unfamiliar text using the main idea graphic organizer. Students then write each statement using a question prompt sentence frame.	Utilizing familiar and unfamiliar text, students share key details in storyboard format with captions and incorporated text features.

Learning target			
I can explain how key details support the topic and purpose.	Teachers revisit the pictures or icon cards with text that was used to organize key details with main idea topic statements. Have students orally explain how each picture or icon matches the main idea statement. Students may use sentence stems or a word bank to support their conversations. Students read short texts and review provided main idea statements and key details for each text. Lead discussion about how each key detail met the supporting criteria. Students use the determined key details in the text box graphic organizer to relate how each detail supports the topic and purpose.	Students create a graphic organizer with key details and explain how they support the main idea.	Students determine which details could be eliminated from the text and not change the meaning or confuse the reader. Students write an additional detail to support the stated topic and purpose.
I can support my thinking with text evidence.	Teachers reference a graphic organizer for determining key details. Teachers provide a bank of quotes and phrases from text. Students eliminate evidence that does not support or match the topic or purpose statement. Students complete a "Match or Does Not Match" T-chart to list reasons why the evidence does or does not match as guided practice. Students apply all the scaffolded supports with new text. Reading support for grade-level text access is provided.	Students reference the graphic organizer for determining key details and explaining how they support the main idea. Students complete a "Where Does It Say That?" activity to find appropriate text. Students apply all the scaffolded supports with new text. Reading support for grade-level text access is provided.	Students find quotes and phrases from multiple texts on the same topic to support key detail statements. Students read complex texts and complete a "My Thinking Text Evidence" chart.

Source for standard: NGA & CCSSO, 2010; Source: ©2023 Wonderview School District. Adapted with permission.

FIGURE 5.11: Learning target response plan for essential learning.

Get Going or Get Better

As you think about your systems and structures to support literacy teams in ensuring that all students are reading at high levels, what changes, refinements, or complete overhauls would help teams systematically provide interventions and extensions? Use the reproducible "Get Going on Chapter 5: Support Systematically With Targeted Acceleration, Interventions, and Extensions" as a reflection tool for the learning in chapter 5 to move forward in the collaborative work of literacy teams.

Get Going on Chapter 5:
Support Systematically With Targeted Acceleration, Interventions, and Extensions

» Are your interventions and extensions systematic or left up to each individual teacher? Are the interventions aligned with your essential standards so that students are getting additional time and support on what teams have determined are the most important skills to support reading achievement?

» How does your team reassess students so that you not only know which students need interventions and extensions, but you also can monitor the effectiveness of your interventions and flexibly regroup if students have improved as a result of the additional time and support?

» Does your team use a protocol to monitor student progress across time, and are there manageable structures for all the adults who work with a student to communicate about the goals and strategies being employed both in the classroom and in intervention?

» Are all students who need additional time and support, be it intervention or extension, included in your response plan, or do you spend so much time focusing on the students who are not yet proficient that you never get around to talking about the needs of students who need extension?

Getting Started?	Getting Better?
We have never worked with a school that stuck with the exact same model of interventions and extensions from one year to the next. Until there are no longer students in your building who need interventions, you will be revising your system of interventions and extensions to better serve your students. You don't need to wait until next year or until you have the money to order another resource to begin interventions. Get started! Just remember, critical questions one and two come first for a reason. Focus on a small set of essential standards that you want students to master (know), and you've developed quality assessments that give you data (show) on which students need interventions or extensions on which essential skills before you tackle answering critical questions three (grow) and four (glow).	Classroom teachers and interventionists cannot work as independent contractors. While it may not be possible for resource teachers and interventionists who support each grade level to attend all grade-level team collaborative meetings, they do need to be considered part of the extended team at each grade level and work within the team norms. Brian Butler, principal of Mason Crest Elementary, often reminded his staff to make decisions based on what is best for student learning, not based on what is most comfortable for the adults in the building (personal communication, 2016). Part of your system of interventions and extensions is a system of communication, so consider how the adults can get better at communicating about student progress in order to improve student reading achievement.

Afterword

TEAMS Can Transform Literacy Outcomes for Students

We, Jacquie and Paula, have been talking about the need for a book that guides literacy teams through the PLC at Work process since we met in 2015. We thought surely someone credible and renowned, a literacy edu-celebrity, was hard at work writing it. And as we waited, we kept hearing the same message from educators we worked with in campuses across North America. We were told time and again literacy is so complex and overwhelming that teams felt uncertain when trying to embrace the PLC at Work process in that particular content area. Teams didn't know where to start ("Do we just look at reading foundation standards to begin, or also include comprehension standards? And what about listening and speaking standards, which are the basis for literacy?"), so they'd abandon literacy standards and focus on mathematics. If only we had a nickel for every time we heard, "Math is just easier for teams to navigate." We love mathematics. We adore mathematics educators, and their work is vital. But we know that, undeniably, there cannot be school improvement without literacy improvement.

Not only is collaborating around literacy possible, it is of the utmost urgency. The stakes are high. We needed that famous literacy somebody to hurry up and write the book.

In 2019, we attended a training for Solution Tree mathematics and literacy associates who were tasked with building a project implementation plan. We noticed the mathematics folks had content-specific and PLC-aligned resource after

> We know that, undeniably, there cannot be school improvement without literacy improvement.

resource to utilize. We're not going to lie; our literacy crew was a little jealous. At the time, the literacy team of associates had resources that were pulled from the archives of our shared files—work we'd led with teams at various places on their PLC journeys. As we pieced together the tools we'd each developed supporting our campuses and districts, Jacquie turned to Paula and said, "This is why we need that book. If the PLC experts in the room are having to scavenge to find team tools and resources for literacy, I completely understand why teachers would find it nearly impossible."

Jacquie's flight home from the training was delayed for hours, so with the urgency she had felt at the project implementation training still fresh in her mind, she decided she was done waiting for that famous somebody to show up and write what we needed. Inspired and determined, she sat on the tarmac and drafted a table of contents. By the time the plane took off three hours later, she had a completed book proposal. A short time later, Paula got a call from Jacquie: "Paula, we aren't waiting anymore. We're writing the book." And so we did.

Here's what we learned. We wasted a lot of precious time waiting for somebody else to show up. Nobody else is coming. It's you. It's us. We're the experts we've all been waiting for. It's the collective power of people who are mission led and purpose driven that transforms literacy outcomes for students. Literacy is not a program, it is a process—a process of teams engaging in the right work.

> Literacy is not a program, it is a process—a process of teams engaging in the right work.

Our mission was to ensure this book gives you the understanding and tools to guide teams to set that work in motion. It is the most important work we can imagine doing, and we are honored you chose to engage with us through the printed word in the preceding pages in order to transform literacy teaching and learning.

Whether getting started or getting better, teams consider the following.

- *What* do we need to do? Strive to improve how team members collaborate around literacy data to answer the critical questions of learning.

- *Why* do we need to do that? To ensure each student has the literacy knowledge, skills, and dispositions to lead a life of unlimited possibilities.

- *How* will we do it? Teach as if the fate of the world depends on it (because for some students, it does).

And as a final note of gratitude: while there is certainly joy and fulfillment in our work, we know ensuring that all students achieve high levels of literacy can be hard, messy, and daunting. We sincerely could not be more grateful to be persevering shoulder to shoulder with literacy leaders like you to make it happen.

We've got this.

Appendix A
TEAMS Process Protocols

Across the chapters of this book, we have guided teams to answer the four critical questions of learning in the PLC at Work process. As teams move through the teaching-assessing cycle that ensures high levels of learning for all, the focus of their collaborative discussions will shift from deconstructing their essential standards to creating assessments, analyzing data, and planning for targeted instruction. In this appendix, you will find step-by-step guides to support literacy teams as they engage in the collaborative actions at each stage of the TEAMS process.

TEAMS Process Protocol for Deconstructing Essential Standards

Teams engage in the following actions. Use the "TEAMS Process Template: Deconstructing Essential Standards" and "Deconstructing and Reconstructing Essential Learning Targets: Critical Question One (Know)" tools to support your work.

1. **Label** the unit by genre or focus, and list the essential standards that align with this unit. Then copy and paste the primary essential standard into the Essential Standard to Deconstruct box.

2. **Look** at the essential standard vertically. What can we learn about the standard in the grade level below us? Above us? What prerequisite skills will students need to access?

3. **Read** any explanations about the standard in the state or provincial standards document or other curriculum guides. Discuss and record understandings.

4. **Consider** what the team can learn from assessment blueprints or released assessment items.

5. **Pull** nouns and related vocabulary from the standard to list common language teachers will use in instruction and accountable language students will use to share their thinking and learning.

6. **Pull** verbs and related vocabulary from the standard to list skills or behaviors students will demonstrate to show their understanding.

7. **Generate** sentence frames or vocabulary stems around academic vocabulary.

8. **Use** the nouns and verbs list to build learning targets shared as *I can* statements, breaking the essential standard into bite-size pieces for student-friendly learning goals. Start with the simplest targets, and build to the more complex or difficult ones, ending with the overall grade-level task that puts all the pieces together.

9. **Create** questions to assist students in guiding their own thinking and to deepen understanding of each *I can* statement.

10. **Group** *I can* statements into related learning goals to guide instruction and informal assessment or feedback to put some of the smaller pieces together in a way that will make sense in the teaching and learning cycle. Use brackets or highlight in a different color for each grouping.

TEAMS Process Protocol for Building Common Formative Assessments

Teams engage in the following actions. Use the "TEAMS Process Template: Building Common Formative Assessments" and "Building an Assessment Plan by Learning Target: Critical Question Two (Show)" tools to support your work.

1. **Name** the unit by genre or focus, and list the essential standards that will be assessed and the date of the summative unit assessment. Determine the tentative dates for common formative assessments within the unit.

2. **Pace** the teaching, assessing, and response to each learning target within the essential literacy standard by deciding how many days of instruction will be dedicated to each of the learning targets and which learning targets will be included on the common formative assessments.

3. **Align** with available assessment blueprints or released assessment items for expectations of rigor, text complexity, and academic vocabulary and models of assessment questions.

4. **Format** the assessment, choosing the most appropriate method or design in order to have the best opportunity to gain insight on student learning and provide feedback.

5. **Select** appropriate texts to be used if assessing for comprehension, specifically evaluating the text complexity and purpose to be sure students can access the text and show what they comprehend.

6. **Create** or curate the common formative assessment, building the questions, answer stems, tasks, or prompts, or collectively determining which premade or prepublished assessment meets the agreed-on criteria and if it needs to be adapted in any way.

7. **Review** the assessment by having all teachers on the team take the test as if they were students to identify any possible edits or revisions. Have teachers determine the *best* answer choice as a key and the best *incorrect* answer to explain why students would make the error.

8. **Refine** and revise as necessary. Assign individual team members action steps and a timeline for completion if necessary before publishing the assessment.

9. **Determine** how to score the assessment by creating a checklist, proficiency scale, or rubric with clearly articulated success criteria.

10. **Calibrate** the scoring guide, and proactively determine how to assign points, give credit, or make determinations of proficiency. How will the team manage accommodations for students with IEP or 504 eligibility? Will other literacy skills such as grammar and punctuation be measured on this assessment?

TEAMS Process Protocol for Analyzing Data for Evidence of Instructional Effectiveness

Teams engage in the following actions. Use the "TEAMS Process Template: Analyzing Data for Evidence of Instructional Effectiveness" tool to support your work.

1. **Name** the unit by genre or focus, and list the essential standards and learning targets that were assessed.

2. **Celebrate** reading data to determine overall gains and strengths as a grade level and for each class. All classes and students are accounted for.

3. **Discover** overall areas in need of continued support as a grade level and for each class. Ensure all classes and students are accounted for.

4. **Organize** support by student, by learning target, and by level of proficiency (need).

5. **Plan** responses by determining which strategies will be most effective to respond when students do and do not learn.

6. **Claim** strengths, celebrations, or glows specific to literacy instructional practices both as a team and individually. Be generous and specific with celebrations!

7. **Target** areas of need, or grows, specific to literacy instructional practices both as a team and individually. Be intentional and specific when identifying needs.

8. **Learn** what professional learning or support is needed for improved literacy instructional practices both as a team and individually.

9. **Aim** to accomplish goals by aligning data outcomes with literacy SMART, team, or unit goal attainment.

10. **Commit** to actions and next steps to be implemented to meet individual and collective literacy instructional goals.

TEAMS Process Protocol for Monitoring Intervention Progress

Teams engage in the following actions. Use the "Building a Response Plan by Learning Target: Critical Question Three (Grow)", "Path to Proficiency Plan Template", "Targeted Intervention Groups and Goals Template", and "Communicating and Collaborating About Learning in Interventions Template" tools to support your work.

1. **Analyze** students' current strengths and needs.

2. **Determine** the focus-of-intervention area and action steps needed.

3. **Decide** who will meet those needs and when the group fits in the schedule.

4. **Establish** data collection and reassessment measures and dates.

5. **Create** a short-term SMART goal for each intervention group.

6. **Set** the next date for progress monitoring to determine if the goal was met for each student.

7. **Clarify** what all adults working with the student are expected to communicate and in what format they should communicate it.

8. **Plan** targeted lessons with built-in opportunities to collaborate around learning.

9. **Reassess** and monitor progress to determine if the goal was met.

10. **Regroup** for instruction on a new goal, or increase the intensity of intervention.

Appendix B

TEAMS Templates

As literacy teams answer the four critical questions of learning, it is crucial that they engage in meaningful collaborative discussions and that the ideas shared in those discussions are captured and saved in order to build clarity and capacity. In this appendix, we have included templates from throughout this book that teams can use to capture their work at each step of the TEAMS process, but we emphasize the importance of the process over the product. Be sure your team is using a template as a tool to further your work and that filling out the form does not become the work. While compliantly filling out boxes will not change literacy outcomes for students, commitment to the TEAMS process can.

TEAMS Process Template: Deconstructing Essential Standards

1. **Label** unit: All standards in this unit:	Essential standard to deconstruct:
2. **Look** at standard in grade level below:	Standard in grade level above:

Prerequisite skills:

3. **Read** notes in local standards or other curriculum guides and record understandings:

4. **Consider** understandings from assessment blueprints and released assessment items:

5. **Pull** nouns or content in standard (plus related vocabulary):

6. **Pull** verbs or skills in standard (plus related vocabulary):

7. **Generate** sentence frames or vocabulary stems around academic vocabulary:

8. **Use** nouns and verbs to create student-friendly *I can* statements arranged in a learning progression from simple to complex:

9. **Create** guiding questions for *I can* statements:

10. **Group** *I can* statements into related learning goals:

Deconstructing and Reconstructing Essential Learning Targets: Critical Question One (Know)

Unit:			
Essential Literacy Standard:			
Learning Target		**Question One: Know**	**Team Notes**
	→	Instructional strategies? Misconceptions? Appropriate text?	
	→	Instructional strategies? Misconceptions? Appropriate text?	
	→	Instructional strategies? Misconceptions? Appropriate text?	
	→	Instructional strategies? Misconceptions? Appropriate text?	

Building an Assessment Plan by Learning Target:
Critical Question Two (Show)

Unit:			
Essential Literacy Standard:			
Learning Target		**Question Two: Show**	**Team Notes**
	→	How will we assess on common formative assessments? Ideas for quick checks? Appropriate text?	
	→	How will we assess on common formative assessments? Ideas for quick checks? Appropriate text?	
	→	How will we assess on common formative assessments? Ideas for quick checks? Appropriate text?	
	→	How will we assess on common formative assessments? Ideas for quick checks? Appropriate text?	

TEAMS Process Template: Building Common Formative Assessments

<table>
<tr>
<td colspan="4">1. Name unit assessment:
Essential literacy standard assessed:</td>
<td colspan="6">Embedded and recursive essential literacy standards assessed:</td>
</tr>
<tr>
<td colspan="4">Date of common formative assessments:
Date of team data reviews:</td>
<td colspan="6">Date of summative or unit assessment:</td>
</tr>
</table>

2. **Pace** teaching, learning, assessing, and response (essential standard pacing map):

Day 1	Day 2	Day 3	Day 4	Day 5
Day 6	Day 7	Day 8	Day 9	Day 10
Day 11	Day 12	Day 13	Day 14	Day 15

3. **Align** with assessment blueprints by finding examples of the following (check all that apply):

☐ Rigor   ☐ Tasks or behaviors   ☐ Text complexity   ☐ Academic vocabulary

Notes:

4. **Format** assessment design:

Learning target one:

Check all that apply: ☐ Performance   ☐ Selected response   ☐ Constructed response

Notes:

Learning target two:

Check all that apply: ☐ Performance   ☐ Selected response   ☐ Constructed response

Notes:

Learning target three:

Check all that apply: ☐ Performance   ☐ Selected response   ☐ Constructed response

Notes:

5. **Select** text for this assessment:

6. **Create** assessment, ensuring it matches grade-level expectations of the following (check all that apply):

☐ Rigor

☐ Tasks or behaviors

☐ Complexity of text

☐ Academic vocabulary

Link for created or curated assessment:

7. **Review** notes from team observations:

8. **Refine** and revise as needed:

Team member assigned:

9. **Determine** success criteria:

Level 3 descriptors for attaining grade-level proficiency:

Level 2 descriptors for progressing grade-level proficiency:

Level 1 descriptors for emerging grade-level proficiency:

10. **Calibrate** scoring agreements:

Test administration agreements:

Considerations for accommodations:

TEAMS Process Template: Analyzing Data for Evidence of Instructional Effectiveness

Steps 6–10 focus on analyzing data to improve individual and collective practices.

1. **Name** unit assessment: Essential literacy standard assessed:	Embedded and recursive essential literacy standards assessed:

2. **Celebrate** overall student strengths:

3. **Discover** overall student opportunities:

4. **Organize** support by student and by target:

Learning Target One:	Students at Level 1: Emerging	Students at Level 2: Progressing	Students at Level 3: Attaining
Learning Target Two:	Students at Level 1: Emerging	Students at Level 2: Progressing	Students at Level 3: Attaining
Learning Target Three:	Students at Level 1: Emerging	Students at Level 2: Progressing	Students at Level 3: Attaining

5. **Plan** effective actions to accelerate learning:

Effective actions to extend learning:

6. **Claim** overall team strengths:

Individual Teacher Strengths

Teacher one	
Teacher two	
Teacher three	

7. **Target** overall team need:

Individual Teacher Needs	
Teacher one	
Teacher two	
Teacher three	

8. **Learn** overall team professional learning or support needed:

Individual Teacher Professional Learning or Support Needed	
Teacher one	
Teacher two	
Teacher three	

9. **Aim** to achieve goals:

Did we meet our collective goal?

By what margin?

What data do we need to collect to continue to monitor our SMART goal attainment?

How do these data impact upcoming unit goals?

10. **Commit** to next steps:

What actionable commitments do we make as a team?

Actionable Commitments We Make Individually	
Teacher one	
Teacher two	
Teacher three	

Path to Proficiency Plan Template

Student	
Essential Standard	
Learning Targets Focus	
Proficiency Level	Choose one. ☐ Level 1: Emerging grade-level proficiency ☐ Level 2: Progressing grade-level proficiency ☐ Level 3: Attaining grade-level proficiency
Student Strengths	

	Teacher actions:	Student actions:
Action Plan		

Check-In Dates	Date of checkpoint one:	Date of checkpoint two:	Date of checkpoint three:

Proficiency at Checkpoint One	Choose one. ☐ Level 1: Emerging ☐ Level 2: Progressing ☐ Level 3: Attaining	Checkpoint one notes:
Proficiency at Checkpoint Two	Choose one. ☐ Level 1: Emerging ☐ Level 2: Progressing ☐ Level 3: Attaining	Checkpoint two notes:
Proficiency at Checkpoint Three	Choose one. ☐ Level 1: Emerging ☐ Level 2: Progressing ☐ Level 3: Attaining	Checkpoint three notes:

Targeted Intervention Groups and Goals Template

Students in Intervention Group	Classroom Teacher	Intervention Action Steps	Reading Skill Goal	Group Teacher, Timing, and Ratio	Data Collection and Reassessment Date

Systematically Communicating and Collaborating About Learning in Interventions

Reading Group Goal	Focus of Instruction (Learning Target)	Strategies to Share or Questions for Team

Student Name	Notes From Intervention	Notes From Classroom

Building a Response Plan by Learning Target:
Critical Question Three (Grow)

Unit:			
Essential Literacy Standard:			
Learning Target		**Question Three: Grow**	**Team Notes**
	→	What intervention strategies are most effective?	
	→	What intervention strategies are most effective?	
	→	What intervention strategies are most effective?	
	→	What intervention strategies are most effective?	

Building a Response Plan by Learning Target:
Critical Question Four (Glow)

Unit:			
Essential Literacy Standard:			
Learning Target		**Question Four: Glow**	**Team Notes**
	→	What extension strategies will deepen the learning?	
	→	What extension strategies will deepen the learning?	
	→	What extension strategies will deepen the learning?	
	→	What extension strategies will deepen the learning?	

References and Resources

Acceleration. (n.d.). In *Merriam-Webster's online dictionary*. Accessed at www.merriam -webster.com/dictionary/acceleration on January 10, 2023.

Ainsworth, L. (2003). *Power standards: Identifying the standards that matter the most.* Englewood, CO: Advanced Learning Press.

Ainsworth, L. (2013). *Prioritizing the Common Core: Identifying specific standards to emphasize the most.* Englewood, CO: Lead + Learn Press.

Ainsworth, L., & Viegut, D. (2006). *Common formative assessments: How to connect standards-based instruction and assessment.* Thousand Oaks, CA: Corwin Press.

Arkansas Department of Education. (n.d.). *English language arts standards and courses.* Little Rock, AR: Author. Accessed at https://dese.ade.arkansas.gov/Offices/learning -services/curriculum-support/english-language-arts-standards-and-courses on October 7, 2022.

Australian Bureau of Statistics. (2013). *Programme for the International Assessment of Adult Competencies, Australia.* Accessed at www.abs.gov.au/statistics/people /education/programme-international-assessment-adult-competencies-australia /latest-release on January 11, 2023.

Bingham, G. E., & Hall-Kenyon, K. M. (2013). Examining teachers' beliefs about and implementation of a balanced literacy framework. *Journal of Research in Reading, 36*(1), 14–28.

Black, P., & Wiliam, D. (2010). Inside the black box: Raising standards through classroom assessment. *Phi Delta Kappan, 92*(1). https://doi.org/10.1177 /003172171009200119

Blankenship, J. (2013, November 8). Functional illiteracy continues to grow, but there is help. *Beckley Register-Herald.* Accessed at https://beckleyregisterherald.newspaper archive.com/beckley-register-herald/2013-11-08/page-4 on October 7, 2022.

Brookhart, S. M. (2019). Feedback and measurement. In S. M. Brookhart & J. H. McMillan (Eds.), *Classroom assessment and educational measurement* (pp. 64–78). Abingdon-on-Thames, England: Routledge.

Buffum, A., Mattos, M., & Malone, J. (2018). *Taking action: A handbook for RTI at Work.* Bloomington, IN: Solution Tree Press.

Buffum, A., Mattos, M., & Weber, C. (2010). The why behind RTI. *Educational Leadership, 68*(2), 10–16.

Buffum, A., Mattos, M., & Weber, C. (2012). *Simplifying response to intervention: Four essential guiding principles.* Bloomington, IN: Solution Tree Press.

Butler, S., Urrutia, K., Buenger, A., Gonzalez, N., Hunt, M., & Eisenhart, C. (2010). (Eds.). *A review of the current research on vocabulary instruction.* Washington, DC: National Reading Technical Assistance Center. Accessed at www2.ed.gov/programs /readingfirst/support/rmcfinal1.pdf on January 11, 2023.

Carroll, T. (2009). The next generation of learning teams. *Phi Delta Kappan, 91*(2), 8–13.

Chang, J. (2011). A case study of the "Pygmalion effect": Teacher expectations and student achievement. *International Education Studies, 4*(1), 198–201.

Chappuis, J. (2014). *Seven strategies of assessment for learning* (2nd ed.). Boston: Pearson.

Clarke, M., & Bordonaro, K. M. (2022, June). *Inclusive practices* [Workshop]. Solution Tree Summit on PLC at Work, Lincolnshire, IL.

Collaboration. (n.d.). In *Merriam-Webster's online dictionary.* Accessed at www.merriam -webster.com/dictionary/collaboration on June 5, 2022.

Collective efficacy. (n.d.). In *Hattie ranking: 252 influences and effect sizes related to student achievement.* Accessed at https://visible-learning.org/hattie-ranking -influences-effect-sizes-learning-achievement on January 30, 2023.

Conzemius, A. E., & O'Neill, J. (2014). *The handbook for SMART school teams: Revitalizing best practices for collaboration* (2nd ed.). Bloomington, IN: Solution Tree Press.

Curtis, C. P. (2013). *The Watsons go to Birmingham—1963.* New York: Yearling.

Darling-Hammond, L., Hyler, M. E., & Gardner, M. (2017, June). *Effective teacher professional development.* Palo Alto, CA: Learning Policy Institute. Accessed at https://learningpolicyinstitute.org/sites/default/files/product-files/Effective _Teacher_Professional_Development_REPORT.pdf on December 22, 2022.

DeLong, T. J. (2011, August 4). Three questions for effective feedback. *Harvard Business Review.* Accessed at https://hbr.org/2011/08/three-questions-for-effective-feedback on January 11, 2023.

Dempsey, K. (2017, July 19). *Does your school have a guaranteed and viable curriculum? How would you know?* Denver, CO: McREL. Accessed at www.mcrel.org /does-your-school-have-a-guaranteed-and-viable-curriculum on October 7, 2022.

Dimich, N. (2015). *Design in five: Essential phases to create engaging assessment practice.* Bloomington, IN: Solution Tree Press.

Donohoo, J. (2017). *Collective efficacy: How educators' beliefs impact student learning.* Thousand Oaks, CA: Corwin.

DuFour, R. (2008, December 9). *Clarifying collective inquiry* [Blog post]. Accessed at www.allthingsplc.info/blog/view/40/Clarifying+Collective+Inquiry on October 5, 2020.

DuFour, R. (2009). *Servant leadership: What is a team?* [Video file]. Accessed at Global PD Teams at https://app.globalpd.com/search/content/MTI5NQ== on February 2, 2023.

DuFour, R. (2015). *In praise of American educators: And how they can become even better.* Bloomington, IN: Solution Tree Press.

DuFour, R. (2016a, August 17). *Building the solid foundation of a Professional Learning Community at Work* [Conference presentation]. Professional Learning Communities at Work Institute, Milwaukee, WI.

DuFour, R. (2016b, Summer). Loose vs tight. *AllThingsPLC Magazine, 1*(1), 33.

DuFour, R., DuFour, R., Eaker, R., Many, T. W., & Mattos, M. (2016). *Learning by doing: A handbook for Professional Learning Communities at Work* (3rd ed.). Bloomington, IN: Solution Tree Press.

DuFour, R., & Marzano, R. J. (2011). *Leaders of learning: How district, school, and classroom leaders improve student achievement.* Bloomington, IN: Solution Tree Press.

Eaker, R., Hagadone, M., Keating, J., & Rhoades, M. (2021). *Leading PLCs at Work districtwide: From boardroom to classroom.* Bloomington, IN: Solution Tree Press.

Ebert, K. D., & Scott, C. M. (2016). Bringing the Simple View of Reading to the clinic: Relationships between oral and written language skills in a clinical sample. *Journal of Communication Disorders, 62,* 147–160.

Embedded. (n.d.). In *Dictionary.com*. Accessed at www.dictionary.com/browse /embedded on January 30, 2023.

Enrichment. (n.d.). In *Collins online dictionary*. Accessed at www.collinsdictionary.com /us/dictionary/english/enrich on January 30, 2023.

Extension. (n.d.). In *Merriam-Webster's online dictionary*. Accessed at www.merriam -webster.com/dictionary/extension on October 6, 2022.

Fine, E. H. (1999). *Under the lemon moon*. New York: Lee & Low Books.

Goddard, R. D., Hoy, W. K., & Hoy, A. W. (2004). Collective efficacy beliefs: Theoretical developments, empirical evidence, and future directions. *Educational Researcher, 33*(3), 3–13.

Gough, P. B., & Tunmer, W. E. (1986). Decoding, reading, and reading disability. *Remedial and Special Education, 7*(1), 6–10.

Green, E. L., & Goldstein, D. (2019, October 30). Reading scores on national exam decline in half the states. *The New York Times*. Accessed at www.nytimes .com/2019/10/30/us/reading-scores-national-exam.html on October 7, 2022.

Harris, T. L., & Hodges, R. E. (Eds.). (1995). *The literacy dictionary: The vocabulary of reading and writing*. Newark, DE: International Reading Association.

Hasbrouck, J. (n.d.). *Developing fluent readers*. Accessed at www.readingrockets.org /article/developing-fluent-readers on October 25, 2022.

Hattie, J. A. C. (2012). *Visible learning for teachers: Maximizing impact on learning*. New York: Routledge.

Heller, J. (2020, January 22). *Comprehension challenge* [Blog post]. Accessed at www.allthingsplc.info/blog/view/408/comprehension-challenge on January 22, 2020.

Heshmat, S. (2018, June 29). 10 key elements of successful goal achievement: A guide for setting—and achieving—your long-term goals [Blog post]. *Psychology Today*. Accessed at www.psychologytoday.com/us/blog/science-choice/201806/10-key -elements-successful-goal-achievement on January 11, 2023.

Hopping, L. J. (1995). *Wild weather: Hurricanes!* New York: Scholastic.

Intervention. (n.d.). In *Merriam-Webster's online dictionary*. Accessed at www.merriam -webster.com/dictionary/intervention on October 7, 2022.

Jackson, A., & Patankar, A. (2013, February 8). Collective inquiry. *Education Week*. Accessed at www.edweek.org/teaching-learning/opinion-collective-inquiry/2013/02 on October 6, 2022.

Jacobs, C. (2020, January 3). Why teachers should avoid labelling students and instead have high expectations for all. *TES Magazine*. Accessed at www.tes.com /magazine/archived/why-teachers-should-avoid-labelling-students-and-instead-have -high-expecations on November 11, 2022.

Jenkins, K. (2003). *The potato chip man and other stories*. Bloomington, IN: Xlibris.

Kerr, D., Hulen, T. A., Heller, J., & Butler, B. K. (2021). *What about us? The PLC at Work process for preK–2 teams*. Bloomington, IN: Solution Tree Press.

Kim, J. S. (2008). Research and the reading wars. *Phi Delta Kappan, 89*(5), 372–375.

Kramer, S. V., & Schuhl, S. (2017). *School improvement for all: A how-to guide for doing the right work*. Bloomington, IN: Solution Tree Press.

Lencioni, P. (2010). *The five dysfunctions of a team: A leadership fable* (20th anniversary ed.). San Francisco: Jossey-Bass.

Linchpin. (n.d.). In *Collins online dictionary*. Accessed at www.collinsdictionary.com/us /dictionary/english/linchpin on February 1, 2023.

Lonigan, C. J., & Milburn, T. F. (2017). Identifying the dimensionality of oral language skills of children with typical development in preschool through fifth grade. *Journal of Speech, Language, and Hearing Research, 60*(8), 2185–2198.

Lovett, M. C. (2013). Make exams worth more than the grade: Using exam wrappers to promote metacognition. In M. Kaplan, N. Silver, D. Lavaque-Manty, & D. Meizlish (Eds.), *Using reflection and metacognition to improve student learning: Across the disciplines, across the academy* (pp. 18–52). Sterling, VA: Stylus.

Lower, S. (n.d.). *3.4: Classifying matter according to its composition*. Accessed at https:// chem.libretexts.org/Bookshelves/Introductory_Chemistry/Map%3A_Introductory _Chemistry_(Tro)/03%3A_Matter_and_Energy/3.04%3A_Classifying_Matter _According_to_Its_Composition on October 27, 2022.

Many, T. W., & Horrell, T. (2014). Prioritizing the standards using R.E.A.L. criteria. *TEPSA News, 71*(1). Accessed at https://absenterprisedotcom.files.wordpress .com/2016/06/real-standards.pdf on January 16, 2023.

Marzano, R. J. (2003). *What works in schools: Translating research into action*. Alexandria, VA: ASCD.

Marzano, R. J. (2018). *Making classroom assessments reliable and valid*. Bloomington, IN: Solution Tree Press.

Marzano, R. J., Yanoski, D. C., Hoegh, J. K., & Simms, J. A. (2013). *Using Common Core standards to enhance classroom instruction and assessment*. Bloomington, IN: Marzano Resources.

Mattos, M. (2021). *Building the pyramid: How to create a highly effective, multitiered system of supports* [Keynote address]. Solution Tree RTI at Work Institute, San Antonio, TX.

Moss, C. M., Brookhart, S. M., & Long, B. A. (2011). Knowing your learning target. *Educational Leadership, 68*(6), 66–69.

Muhammad, A. (2014). *Solution Tree Summit on PLC at Work* [Keynote address]. Phoenix, AZ.

Munson, D. (2000). *Enemy pie.* San Francisco: Chronicle Books.

Murawski, W. W., & Lochner, W. W. (2011). Observing co-teaching: What to ask for, look for, and listen for. *Intervention in School and Clinic, 46*(3), 174–183.

National Center for Education Statistics. (2022). *Nation's report card: Reading.* Accessed at https://nces.ed.gov/nationsreportcard/reading on October 10, 2022.

National Governors Association Center for Best Practices & Council of Chief State School Officers. (2010). *Common Core State Standards for English language arts and literacy in history/social studies, science, and technical subjects.* Washington, DC: Authors. Accessed at www.corestandards.org/assets/CCSSI_ELA%20Standards.pdf on October 6, 2022.

National Reading Panel. (2000). *Teaching children to read: An evidence-based assessment of the scientific research literature on reading and its implications for reading instruction—Reports of the subgroups.* Bethesda, MD: National Institute of Child Health and Human Development. Accessed at www.nichd.nih.gov/sites/default/files/publications/pubs/nrp/Documents/report.pdf on October 10, 2022.

Nietzel, M. T. (2020, September 9). Low literacy levels among U.S. adults could be costing the economy $2.2 trillion a year. *Forbes.* Accessed at www.forbes.com/sites/michaeltnietzel/2020/09/09/low-literacy-levels-among-us-adults-could-be-costing-the-economy-22-trillion-a-year/?sh=775191454c90 on October 6, 2022.

Orton Gillingham Online Academy. (2017). *Illiteracy statistics in the United States.* Accessed at https://ortongillinghamonlinetutor.com/illiteracy-statistics-in-the-united-states on October 10, 2022.

Pallotta, J. (2018). *Ultimate jungle rumble: Who would win?* New York: Scholastic.

Paris, S., & Hamilton, E. (2014). The development of children's reading comprehension. In S. E. Israel (Ed.), *Handbook of research on reading comprehension* (pp. 56–77). Abingdon-on-Thames, England: Routledge.

Petersen, D. (2002). *Petrified Forest National Park.* New York: Children's Press.

Piercy, M. (1982). *Circles on the water.* New York: Knopf.

Prevention. (n.d.). In *Merriam-Webster's online dictionary.* Accessed at www.merriam-webster.com/dictionary/prevention on January 23, 2023.

Reading Horizons. (n.d.). *Reading wars: Phonics vs. whole language instruction.* Accessed at www.readinghorizons.com/reading-strategies/teaching/phonics-instruction/reading-wars-phonics-vs-whole-language-reading-instruction on October 10, 2022.

Reading Rockets. (n.d.a). *Accommodations and modifications*. Accessed at www.readingrockets.org/article/accommodations-and-modifications on December 28, 2022.

Reading Rockets. (n.d.b). *Phonological and phonemic awareness*. Accessed at www .readingrockets.org/helping/target/phonologicalphonemic on October 25, 2022.

Recursive. (n.d.). In *Collins online unabridged English dictionary*. Accessed at www .collinsdictionary.com/us/dictionary/english/recursive on December 18, 2022.

Reeves, D. B. (2013). *Making standards work: How to implement standards-based assessments in the classroom, school, and district* (3rd ed.). Boston: Houghton Mifflin Harcourt.

Research. (n.d.). In *Cambridge English dictionary*. Accessed at https://dictionary .cambridge.org/us/dictionary/english/research on December 17, 2022.

Rose, J. (2006, March). *Independent review of the teaching of early reading: Final report*. Annesley, Nottingham, England: Department for Education and Skills. Accessed at https://dera.ioe.ac.uk/5551/2/report.pdf on October 5, 2022.

Rosenthal, R., & Jacobson, L. (1968). Pygmalion in the classroom. *The Urban Review, 3*, 16–20.

Scarborough, H. S. (2001). Connecting early language and literacy to later reading (dis)abilities: Evidence, theory, and practice. In S. B. Neuman & D. K. Dickinson (Eds.), *Handbook for early literacy research* (pp. 97–110). New York: Guilford Press.

Senge, P. M. (1990). *The fifth discipline: The art and practice of the learning organization*. New York: Doubleday.

Shanahan, T. (2020). What constitutes a science of reading instruction? *Reading Research Quarterly, 55*(S1), S235–S247.

Silverstein, S. (1974). *Where the sidewalk ends: The poems and drawings of Shel Silverstein*. New York: Harper & Row.

Statistics Canada. (2015). *Literacy, numeracy: Average scores and distribution of proficiency levels, by labour force status, highest level of education and age group*. Accessed at www150.statcan.gc.ca/t1/tbl1/en/tv.action?pid=3710004901 on January 11, 2023.

Stiggins, R. (2001). *Student-involved classroom assessment* (3rd ed.). Upper Saddle River, NJ: Merrill Prentice Hall.

Stiggins, R. (2005). From formative assessment to assessment for learning: A path to success in standards-based schools. *Phi Delta Kappan, 87*(4), 324–328.

Systematically. (n.d.). In *Merriam-Webster's online dictionary*. Accessed at www.merriam -webster.com/dictionary/systematic on October 6, 2022.

Team. (n.d.). In *Merriam-Webster's online dictionary*. Accessed at www.merriam-webster .com/dictionary/team on October 7, 2022.

Texas Education Agency. (n.d.). *19 TAC chapter 110: Texas essential knowledge and skills for English language arts and reading.* Accessed at https://tea.texas.gov/about-tea /laws-and-rules/texas-administrative-code/19-tac-chapter-110 on October 6, 2022.

Texas Education Agency. (2017). *STAAR grade 3 reading released (May 2017).* Accessed at https://tea.texas.gov/sites/default/files/STAAR_G3-2017-Test-Read-f.pdf on January 16, 2023.

Texas Education Agency. (2018). *STAAR grade 3 reading released (May 2018).* Accessed at https://tea.texas.gov/sites/default/files/2018_STAAR_Gr3_Reading_Test.pdf on January 16, 2023.

Tschannen-Moran, M., & Barr, M. (2004). Fostering student learning: The relationship of collective teacher efficacy and student achievement. *Leadership and Policy in Schools, 3*(3), 189–209.

The Understood Team. (n.d.). *The difference between accommodations and modifications.* Accessed at www.understood.org/en/articles/the-difference-between -accommodations-and-modifications on December 28, 2022.

Underwood, S. (2018, January). *What is the evidence for an uninterrupted, 90-minute literacy instruction block?* [Brief]. Portland, OR: Education Northwest. Accessed at https://educationnorthwest.org/sites/default/files/resources/uninterrupted-literacy -block-brief.pdf on January 11, 2023.

Walters, A. (2022, March 31). Culture still eats strategy for breakfast. *Industry Week.* Accessed at www.industryweek.com/leadership/corporate-culture/article/21237760 /culture-still-eats-strategy-for-breakfast on November 17, 2022.

White, K. (2019, April 29). *Making strengths (and needs) analysis count in the classroom.* Accessed at https://allthingsassessment.info/2019/04/29/classroom-strengths-and -needs-analysis on January 11, 2023.

White, K. (2022). *Student self-assessment: Data notebooks, portfolios, and other tools to advance learning.* Bloomington, IN: Solution Tree Press.

Wiggins, G., & McTighe, J. (2005). *Understanding by design* (2nd ed.). Alexandria, VA: ASCD.

Zigmond, N., & Magiera, K. (2001, Autumn). A focus on co-teaching. *Current Practice Alerts, 6.* Accessed at http://ppsacademicsupport.weebly.com/uploads/2/9/0/4 /29048495/co-teachinginfo_ld.pdf on October 6, 2022.

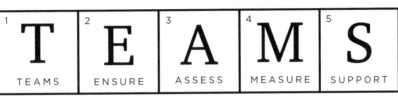

Index

B

C

D

O

oral language, 36, 37, 45, 46, 68, 115

P

pencil-and-paper tasks, 67. *See also* assessing and monitoring achievement with ongoing assessments

performance-based assessments, 67. *See also* assessing and monitoring achievement with ongoing assessments

phonemes, 37

phonemic awareness

   assessment options for consideration form, 68

   critical components of reading and, 36, 37

   literacy and, 3

   proficiency mapping and, 45

phonics

   assessment options for consideration form, 68

   critical components of reading and, 36, 37–38

   literacy and, 3

   phonics assessment wrapper example, 90–91

   proficiency mapping and, 45

   reading wars and, 4–6

PLCs at Work (Professional Learning Communities at Work)

   big ideas of, 8

   critical questions of. *See* critical questions of a PLC

   definition of a PLC, 6–8

   finding joy in the journey, 2–3

   joining the journey, 3

   loose and tight elements of, 10

   reading wars and, 6

   TEAMS and, 10

   understanding, 6–11

practice standards, 41. *See also* essential standards; standards

prevention, 114–115

process standards, 41. *See also* essential standards; standards

Professional Learning Communities at Work. *See* PLCs at Work (Professional Learning Communities at Work)

proficiency mapping

   about, 45

   for the academic year, 47–48

   essential standards and, 58

   example of year-at-a-glance proficiency map by quarter, 48

   examples of path to proficiency plans, 83–84, 84–85

   by grade band, 45–47

   reproducibles for, 155

T

V

W

What About Us?
Diane Kerr, Tracey A. Hulen, Jacqueline Heller, and Brian K. Butler
Early childhood learning is a critical launchpad for every student's social, emotional, and intellectual growth. With *What About Us?* discover how to achieve the full potential of preK–2 classrooms through proven best practices aligned to the PLC at Work® process.
BKF941

Reading and Writing Instruction for PreK Through First-Grade Classrooms in a PLC at Work®
Erica Martin and Lisa May
Prepare your collaborative PLC team to fully support and encourage every learner's literacy development. Written specifically for teachers of preK through first grade, this practical resource includes tools and strategies for designing standards-aligned instruction, assessments, interventions, and more.
BKF901

Reading and Writing Instruction for Second- and Third-Grade Classrooms in a PLC at Work®
Sarah Gord and Kathryn E. Sheridan
Fully prepare students to begin the pivotal transition from learning to read to reading to learn. Written for individual teachers and collaborative teams, this carefully crafted resource outlines a high-quality approach to literacy instruction for second and third grade.
BKF915

Reading and Writing Instruction for Fourth- and Fifth-Grade Classrooms in a PLC at Work®
Kathy Tuchman Glass
Prepare students to succeed with increasingly sophisticated reading and writing challenges. Designed for teachers of grades 4–5, this book fully prepares individuals and collaborative PLC teams to establish a rich and robust plan for quality literacy instruction, assessment, and intervention.
BKF902

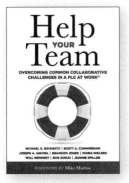

Help Your Team
Michael D. Bayewitz, Scott A. Cunningham, Joseph A. Ianora, Brandon Jones, Maria Nielsen, Will Remmert, Bob Sonju, and Jeanne Spiller
Written by eight PLC at Work® experts, this practical guide addresses the most common challenges facing collaborative teams. Each chapter offers a variety of templates, processes, and strategies to help your team resolve conflict, focus on the right work, and take collective responsibility for student success.
BKF886

Solution Tree | Press — *a division of* Solution Tree

"Tremendous, tremendous, tremendous!

The speaker made me do some very deep internal reflection about the **PLC process** and the personal responsibility I have in making the school improvement process work **for ALL kids.**"

—Marc Rodriguez, teacher effectiveness coach,
Denver Public Schools, Colorado

 PD Services

Our experts draw from decades of research and their own experiences to bring you practical strategies for building and sustaining a high-performing PLC. You can choose from a range of customizable services, from a one-day overview to a multiyear process.

Book your PLC PD today!
888.763.9045

Solution Tree